My Unexpected Journey

Jackie Dobrosky

My Unexpected Journey
Copyright © 2017 by Jackie Dobrosky

Cover by Becky Pourchot

All rights reserved by MRK Publishing

Copy Editor Karen Nicely

190p. ill. cm.

ISBN 978-1-935795-48-3

All Rights Reserved. No part of this book may be reproduced, stored in a retrieval system, or transmitted in any form or by any means, electronic, mechanical, photocopying, recording, or otherwise, without permission in writing from MRK Publishing

MRK Publishing

PO Box 353431

Palm Coast, FL 32135-3431

www.MRKPublishing.com

Printed in the United States of America

I WOULD LIKE TO THANK THE FOLLOWING PEOPLE, WITHOUT WHOSE INSPIRATION AND BELIEF IN ME I WOULD NEVER HAVE BEEN ABLE TO BRING MY STORY TO LIFE:

MICHAEL RAY KING, Acclaimed Author/Mentor/Publisher
Thank you for helping me reach inside myself and find the courage to write my story. You gave me the strength and encouragement to put my life's journey on paper by writing the TRUTH. Without your guidance, I could never have achieved what I set out to accomplish. Thank you for never letting me give up.

KARIN NICELY, Editor
You worked your magic in bringing my words to life and transforming them in such a way that even I was in awe.

BECKY POURCHOT, Cover and Layout Designer

Thank you for designing my cover and for all your help in finding just the right words to inspire readers to read my book.

And especially to my husband Jim, thank you for your encouragement, patience, and belief in me to continue on my journey.

MY UNEXPECTED JOURNEY

What you are about to read is the story of *My Unexpected Journey*, the journey that has put me on the path I walk today. As I look back into my past, it has many twists and turns. It has happiness, a lot of sadness, heartbreak, illness, abuse, and real-life miracles. I would not change one thing about my journey, because I am the woman I am today for having gone through it and surviving. I dedicate this book to all the people who have faced adversities in their own lives. Sometimes we think we are the only ones going through tough times, but we should realize it's just part of the journey, part of what I call *LIFE*. Remember: what doesn't break us makes us stronger.

Through all of this, I have learned to really trust the Lord. If it weren't for His unconditional love for all of us, we would not be here. It is true that some of us face a lot more challenges than others. But then, who are we to say another person's trials are not as large of a challenge to them? Sometimes we feel like we can't go on another day or have another challenge hit us; each of us has our own breaking point. It's up to us to just ask God for strength and for guidance. Just trust with all your heart—the Lord will never let you down. Even when things happen that we feel aren't fair, there is always a reason, and sometimes the message won't become clear to us till years later. But nothing is a coincidence. We are right where we are supposed to be and at this present moment. I am about to share with you my life's journey and hope you find something in it that speaks to you, that inspires you to keep moving forward in your own journey.

God Bless

This true story is dedicated to all those who have experienced adversity, who may now be suffering from pain or loss, and who are searching for a way to not only survive but to accept with thankful hearts all of the challenges and joys along the path of your own unexpected journeys.

CHAPTER 1

When my conscious journey began, I was a small child back in the 1950s, growing up in a middle-class family. I was the oldest of three with a younger brother and a younger sister. It was not a very stable family. All I knew were the day-to-day things of being a child. But for some reason, I have gaps in my memory of my life. And maybe this was my defense mechanism, used to cover up my pain.

My Unexpected Journey

Back in the early 1960s, we kids would play outside for hours in the summer. We were most happy when we could play with friends and escape the drama of my parents' dysfunctional marriage. As small kids, my siblings and I experienced very little happiness. We did what we could to entertain ourselves. If we were good, my mother would take us to see the cows in the country and get us ice cream for fun. We thought that was a great summer night out.

My father was only in our life for thirteen years, off and on. I was raised mostly by my mother. My parents divorced when I was quite young, and I don't have a lot of memories of my father. Even during the times he was with us, he was not in the picture much. However, I do know he was a millworker and that we came from a small steel town in Ohio.

Many of the memories I do have of my father involve his abusive behavior, both physical and mental, toward my mother. All

I can clearly remember of him was his fighting with my mother and beating her. My brother, sister, and I would hide in our bedrooms when they started fighting. We cried. We felt helpless. I remember a time when my brother jumped on my father's back and started hitting him to make him stop hurting our mother. But even though my father beat my mother, he never hit us kids. He also gambled a lot, so our financial situation was never stable. I remember times when there would be hundreds of dollars on the table from his winnings at the track one lucky week while the next week my parents would be fighting over the fact they didn't have money for groceries.

They were very young, uneducated parents, and we children just happened to be part of a whole situation I feel complicated their lives. My mother came from a family of abuse and poverty herself. My parents were kids just raising kids and probably not too happy.

My Unexpected Journey

After our parents eventually divorced, we were shuffled around from house to house with my mother. No sooner did we get settled in one house than we were moving again and going from school to school. In fact, we moved so much—maybe thirty times—that I attended ten different schools. Stability was obviously something I was not familiar with.

I can't even remember certain houses we lived in that corresponded with the schools I attended. It was such a blur. I guess that's when my memory loss began.

I don't remember how long they were divorced before my parents did the utmost insane thing: they remarried. Then they decided to move us to Hollywood, Florida, to start their married life over. That time, my grandfather helped them rent a house. Another school, another house, and more friends to make. As I look back, from what I can remember, I was somewhat happy our family was still together. But we were trapped in that family and had nowhere to go but with them. As the months went by, the fighting started again and didn't stop. My father couldn't keep a job, and his physical and emotional abuse toward my mother were awful.

As with many of my childhood memories, I blocked out much of the time period during which we lived in Florida, so I'm not sure how many years we were there. Maybe that was a good thing. But as time went by, and with intense therapy as an adult, I started remembering my past. I can remember that my parents decided to divorce again, and we moved back to Ohio with my mother. I'm not sure why—maybe she felt she was stuck with us—but my mother became very frustrated, angry, and abusive. I do remember that was the beginning of a very dark time for me. Sometimes I don't think she thought about what she was doing to us as kids. She just did what she wanted, and we didn't have a choice; we just followed and listened.

I didn't know how to handle my life at that time; I was just a kid. So, I ate. I was an overweight child who just wanted to be accepted and loved. So, I ate more. The kids all made fun of me at school, which made me very nervous about being there. I was also very insecure. At lunch, the kids would get together and give me their food at the cafeteria table to see how much I could eat. It was like a game, and I went along with the joke because I thought they liked me and wanted to be my friends. And since food was already my friend, I ate everything they gave me. I guess it gave me comfort. And a false sense of the acceptance I wanted so badly. In the end, it left me more insecure and feeling even worse about myself. Why didn't the other kids like me? I was always kind and helpful to everyone.

With no money after our return from Florida, my mother and three of us had to live with my grandparents, who were not wealthy. Grandma came from a farm and was a little rough around the edges. Grandpa, on the other hand, was a mild soul. He was a barber by trade, and by the time we lived with them I don't think he worked any more. He did have a very large garden in the back yard, though. Oh, did he love his garden! It truly was amazing. Grandma loved planting her flowers; marigolds were her favorite. They didn't have much, but what they had they shared with us. We never went hungry. Their house was a five-hundred-square-foot, one-bedroom home with the bathroom in its very scary basement, where spiderwebs gathered in the beams. It was always dark, and it smelled moldy. Along with showering and bathing in the basement, we had to sleep there as well on cots set up for us kids right next to the furnace. And let me tell you, it was a frightening place to sleep. This was not a cozy, remodeled basement, but we had no choice. I still can remember the sound of the creepy furnace and the smell of the moldy bathroom surrounding me as I cried myself to sleep each night in that place.

Now comes the best part. My aunt was also getting a divorce at the time and with the same situation, so—you guessed it—my cousin also stayed in the basement with us. I guess our mothers slept upstairs on the couch.

At that point, we began attending another school. I think it was the sixth school I had attended, and I had just started middle school.

We moved so many times after Grandma's basement stay. First it was houses my mother rented close to Grandma's. We had furniture that was given to us, and at that time we could have our own bedrooms. But as winter set in, the money was slim and I remember a time we had to burn some of our furniture in the fireplace to stay warm because our heat had been shut off.

We didn't last at that particular house very long. Although they were divorced, my father, who had also moved back to Ohio when we did and was now living with his parents, was still torturing my mother. I remember a time all three of us and my mother hid in the attic to get away from him when he broke into the house. We sat in that cold, scary, foul-smelling attic, hiding while he was trying to find us—mostly her. Again, I don't remember him ever beating us, just her, but the trauma of that time sticks in my head today. Three kids scared to death of what was to happen.

Well, since my mother could not afford the rent there, that residence didn't last long and we moved again, this time to an apartment across town. It was far from our grandparents' house, and we missed being close to them. It had been comforting to at least know they had been nearby when we lived at the other house, and they always let us hang out with them while my mother worked at a local department store. We were next in a small apartment in Kennedy Park Terrace. Oh, the memories of that apartment were the worst of my childhood. I don't know what happened to my mother at that time, but she became very stressed, mean, and basically unhinged. My memories of that are vague to say the least. As I stated earlier, I blocked things out of my mind as a defense mechanism in order to be able to adapt. I tried to block out the pain, the crying, and the unhappiness. The time in that apartment was another very dark time filled with sadness.

We never spoke about our feelings; we weren't allowed. We became very good at hiding the proverbial elephant in the room. Believe me, after years of living this life, you get so good at the game. We lived in that apartment a very short time before we got evicted and had to move on again.

Mother rented yet another house, this time one close to the home of my favorite aunt. In fact, the back yards connected so we could run back and forth all the time between the homes, and we were happy once again to have family nearby. My mother got a job as a secretary, having to ride the bus to work because she didn't have a car. We went to another school and had to adjust, as usual, to our new life. Mother was a very confused, disturbed woman then, and as I look back, I think she was afraid and didn't know how to show it. She felt she had to show strength all the time, and I think it was all too much for her to handle. She probably did the best she thought she could, but we were just kids; we were afraid, unsure of own lives, and we didn't know what to do to make her happy.

I can't tell you how happy my siblings and I were when we lived by Aunt Margie. I was entering high school, then, and I spent so much of my time at her home. She was a great person, and she loved my brother, my sister, and me, and I loved my cousins, too. We were at Aunt Margie's house every day. I would often stay just to help her with her kids, who were much younger than me. Aunt Margie's house was the one all the kids loved to go to; it was a happy place, and we loved being part of that happiness.

When we had to go home after my mother got off work, we never quite knew how she was going to be feeling. It was like walking on eggshells. We were always being told how much our real father didn't want anything to do with us, and that hurt my heart. I do remember times when he said he would pick us up but never came. I will never know the real reason he never wanted us; he's dead now. I had to put it to rest and believe what she told us. Not only was I suffering from being abandoned by my father, I was left to be raised by my mother alone.

One summer weekend while my mother was going through her divorce, she went on a short holiday with a friend. That same weekend, she met the man who would become our new stepfather.

Jackie Dobrosky

We met him a few weeks after their first meeting, and we loved him the first day we met him. He was amazing, and he made my mother smile again. Once he entered our lives, things brightened up for all of us. Mother was a new woman. He was a former Marine and very structured, yet he was the kindest person I think I ever met in my life. He sat for hours, talking with us and showing us how to do homework. He worked out with my brother to help him lose weight. His idea of discipline was for us to write a page from the encyclopedia. Now, I'm not going to say that was fun, but there was something to this form of discipline. First, it sucked to write a whole page on a Saturday afternoon, and second, we couldn't cheat because after we had written the page, he made us tell him what it was about. We learned real fast that was not how we wanted to spend our weekends, so we tried to stay out of trouble. And yet, no matter how many cramps my fingers had from writing, it was better than getting beaten by my mother.

I think they married a couple months after her divorce was final. We thought we'd struck gold. A new dad and a happy mother. What else could a kid ask for? Well, I think they were only married maybe six months before my mother got pregnant. My half sister Christine was born on my sixteenth birthday. She was a little doll, and we loved her so much. Everyone spoiled her.

A few months after Christine was born, my mother and stepfather had an idea of moving to Florida again. *What?* I am sure that was my mother's idea, just as it had been when we were with my father. So we packed up and left for Florida again but to a different area of the state than where we'd lived previously. Sometimes I wonder if she ever thought of what the relocating might do to us kids, moving around like we did. But I think they were both just thinking about how they could start a new life together, and if it meant taking the kids with them, oh well, we had to adjust. I was about to enter my junior year of high school. There were times, growing up, I didn't know if I was coming or going! Just when things started to settle in, we would up and leave. I can't remember the sequence of the houses and schools, but I counted ten schools all together before I graduated high school. I had just finished up two years of high school in Ohio, and now I was to finish high school in Florida and make friends all over again.

My mother and stepfather rented a very small apartment for all of us to stay in. As usual, we started to attend another school and tried to fit it and make friends, as our routine went. By now, we knew how to play the game; "This is just a pit stop," we would say. We ended up moving three times in the two years we lived in Florida. How is that a healthy way for kids to adjust in life? After living in an apartment, we rented a house for a short time, then that didn't work out, so they rented another house that we lived in until my graduation

My Unexpected Journey

The day after my graduation, in 1974, we moved again, this time back to Ohio once more. I guess they couldn't financially make it in Florida and thought their prospects would be better in Ohio. There they rented a very small house, which we lived in for six months, and then they moved us again. That would be the last house I would live in with my mother and stepfather. I was so *done*. I wanted to start my own life, one that had some stability. I knew from my friends that people had lives in which they didn't move every year or two. I wanted that for a family I would have someday. I was afraid to stand on my own two feet, though. In fact, I didn't even think I could. But after we moved that second time, I plotted a way to get out of that house. At that point, my stepfather was working a lot, my mother was always suffering with back problems, and I finally figured a way out.

Here comes another twist.

CHAPTER 2

When I moved back to Ohio, I reconnected with a good friend named Kathy, who I'd stayed in touch with through my many moves. She began dating a guy who I thought was kind of cute. It was the 1970s, and he always dressed in polyester bell bottoms and silk shirts. *Your typical disco dancer,* I thought. He reminded me of Tony Orlando. I was impressed and asked Kathy if he had a brother, so Kathy set up a way for me to meet his brother, Joe. The only problem with the situation was that Joe didn't speak English. He was from the

Middle East and had only been in our country for six months. It was a weird situation for sure, but Joe was a kind, sort of quirky guy who was not my type at all. We had zero in common, and how we communicated is beyond me. But we dated, and after about six months of dating, he asked me to marry him. Ok, now comes the good part. No, I was not pregnant. I had no good reason and don't know why I would marry into a culture like his, but I did.

I was only nineteen when I married him, and I think it was my way out of a very dysfunctional home life. I look back and wish I had known what I know today; I would have handled things so much differently. I just knew I had to get out of my mother's house and that was my way out. I didn't have a lot of confidence in myself that I could do it on my own. So getting married was the only thing I knew could work. I was following in my mother's footsteps and didn't realize it at the time. She was only eighteen when she was married, and there I was, only nineteen and doing the same thing but with a man who didn't even speak English and was from a Middle Eastern country.

Choices. Oh, those life choices.

We actually had a very traditional wedding on Valentine's Day in 1976. Joe was a Catholic and so was I. We married in his church. At that time, my family did not have a lot of money. My stepdad was working a couple of jobs, and my mother still was plagued by her back condition. I knew the money was very tight and they were able to contribute only a little to the wedding, so Joe and I paid for most of it. Back then, I felt slighted because I never realized till later just how hard they'd had it financially. I just felt like it wasn't fair for us to have to pay for most of the wedding. It wasn't until I returned from my honeymoon that I found out they had given us their last dime and had their gas shut off as a result. It was the dead of winter. I knew then they had given us all they had, and for that I will never forget their love and commitment. To add to everything else, at my wedding, my mother found out she was pregnant with another child. *Oh my God, why?* They could hardly make ends meet. And why would she have another baby at her age? I was just glad to be on my own. My life was finally my own, and I could build it the way I chose.

As I look back on that part of my life, I was just a kid in all respects, doing exactly what my own mother had done, marrying young and having babies. My first child, a girl, was born when I was twenty-one. The second, a boy, was born when I was twenty-three.

Joe and I didn't have much money, but I must say we loved each other, as crazy as that sounds. I was so hungry for a normal life and wanted to do things differently than my mother had. I was going to prove I could and would have a healthy family despite my dysfunctional upbringing.

We also bought our first house when I was twenty-one. Wow, I owned my own home! That was a first for me. Growing up, all we lived in was rentals. Finally, it was my own house with my own family. Life was great; I was happy. I stayed home for four years after the kids were born, and things we very normal. Every Sunday, we went to church and then to the in-laws' for lunch. *Now this is how a real family is supposed to live,* I thought to myself.

I still saw my mother on occasion but not often. She was always having health problems and then dealing with her pregnancy with another sister. She spent a good amount of time in bed because of her back. My youngest half sister and my daughter are only one year apart. In some ways, my two sisters (from my mother's new marriage) and my own kids grew up more like cousins because they were so close in age.

After about four years, Joe and I were eventually able to sell our first home for a profit and buy a nicer, bigger home. *Now that's progress,* I thought. The kids were ready to start school, and things were going so great. My new house was two blocks from my parents' house, so my sisters would often come to our house daily. My kids had a nice park-like back yard with a swing set and huge playhouse. I now had the house like my Aunt Margie had, the house where the kids wanted to play and hang out.

By that time, my husband was offered a job at a company where my stepdad worked. We were already doing well financially, but the new job paid even better. I was still staying home with the kids—until another twist to my life appeared. I was now faced with evidence that Joe was messing around with a woman at his job. My dad, along with the supervisors, had all the evidence in the world that Joe was having an affair with one of the secretaries. He was busted, but because I wanted a family so badly and wanted to keep mine together no matter what, Joe convinced me it was a lie and I allowed myself to believe him. The fiasco did cost him his job, however, so being without a job and having a new home, a mortgage, and two small children brought on a lot of stress.

He eventually found an opportunity to take over an old bar his uncle owned. I didn't want to own or run a bar, especially that one; we didn't even drink in those days. It was a dump, but Joe convinced me the venture was the only way we were going to be able to keep the house. I hated the idea. We had no experience running a business, let alone a bar.

Growing up, I had been used to always following directions and never wanting to disturb things. And yes, I still was great at hiding that *elephant*, the looming problems that I did not want to face or want others to know about. So I did what I knew was the wrong thing. Why? Because

I wanted to keep my family together and never have my children grow up the way I did, I sacrificed my own feelings for theirs. Isn't that what a good mother does, puts the children first?

Ok, here comes another twist in this journey of mine, just when I thought everything was going well once again. We bought the bar, but with my husband not being a United States citizen, I had to put the bar and liquor license in my name. I was now legally responsible for everything that went on in that bar. The problem was I didn't run it; Joe did. He called the shots. I could only run the kitchen, so I put my two kids in daycare when my son was two years old and my daughter was four, and I worked daily from nine till three. Joe ran the bar while I was building the lunch business. I would offer a special of the day and different sandwiches and so forth—mostly just bar food. It was a small bar, not fancy, and I ran the kitchen alone, never being allowed behind the bar. I followed directions. He was my husband; I thought he would do the right thing. I had never run a business before and knew nothing about a bar, anyway.

My husband's hours at the bar were horrendous. He would be there from eight in the morning till three the next morning. Eventually he hired someone to take shifts, but it seemed he always wanted to be there, too, which started to put a strain on our marriage. As he became less and less involved with the kids and me, I found myself alone a lot.

Time went by, and the business was not making the amount of profit we needed. It was just a little bar located close to the mills. The common thing for the patrons, mostly millworkers, to order was a shot and a beer, which cost no more than a buck and a quarter. Our day crowd was made up of the old timers, who started to arrive around eight or nine in the morning and stayed till sometime in the afternoon, also ordering inexpensive items. Therefore, we couldn't make much profit from what either the millworkers or the old timers ordered and Joe decided to find a way to bring in extra money.

What I didn't realize was he would be making that extra money illegally. He hooked up with some vending company that had poker machines. Yes, poker machines are considered gambling because they pay out if a player wins. Back in the mid-1980s, that was illegal in Ohio. We were paid a lot of money to keep the machines in our establishment, and therefore we didn't feel the pinch from not getting as much profit from running the bar. Every time I expressed my concerns about having the poker machines, I was thrown a hundred dollars by the vendor and told to buy the kids something. I was getting sucked into my husband's greedy scheme and began to be good at turning a blind eye to what was going on.

Jackie Dobrosky

I had put myself in a position I knew couldn't end up well, but I take full responsibility for allowing it. Once again, I was used to hiding the *elephant*. No, I didn't want to fail at our business or marriage. I wanted to show everyone we had a great family—in fact, a perfect family. I was only kidding myself, of course. And as time went by, things only escalated. First, I was compensated for keeping quiet about the poker machines. Then, one day, Joe surprised me and brought home a brand-new Cadillac Eldorado as a gift for me. I was amazed. I was only twenty-six years old. I owned my own business, owned my house, had two beautiful kids, and was happy in my marriage. I thought I had it all. Now I had a shiny new Cadillac, too. Wow! How impressive I felt. I was floating on air, so to speak. I knew everyone would be envying me for sure.

Before I knew it, I noticed some shady people in the bar and actions happening with merchandise coming in and out of the business. When I questioned my husband, I was told he'd just bought some things from a customer who needed money. *Oh well,* I thought. *Wlhat harm can that bring?* But soon, Joe was storing merchandise in the basement of the bar. When things got too big, he then started to store them in our garage at our house. Then it got wild. We no longer had a garage for our cars. Instead, it was like a warehouse full of hot items. You name it; we had it—snowmobiles, tires, snow blowers, tools, etc. Certainly too much to mention. I was now even more involved with illegal stuff. Not only did I have gaming machines at the business paying off big dollars, but now I had these people coming to my house like a garage sale, only they came exclusively at night.

Along with things starting to get out of control with the hot merchandise, Joe was spending less and less time at home. I became suspicious and decided to take a ride down to the bar one summer night after I got the kids settled in bed and scheduled a babysitter. I showed up unannounced to find my husband getting very cozy with a woman at the bar. When I approached them, he backed off and explained that she was just a friend's wife out with her girlfriends for a few drinks. People often say to follow your gut—my gut was screaming "liar." I sat next to the woman and her friend and ordered a drink. Joe was quite surprised as we never drank in our bar. Those were the rules, but heck, I wasn't working. I was just a customer at that point.

Things got very chilly then. Joe, acting like he was busy, didn't come down to my end of the bar. He avoided both the woman and me. I tried talking to her, but she was very cold and kept talking to her girlfriend. Bingo. Something was going on. I finished my drink and left with not a word said. I had to get home to my kids. The next day, Joe said nothing when I came into work. As with everything else, he felt he was the man and I was to follow orders and accept what I was told. You must remember his culture, too. He was from the Middle East, where men felt women did not tell men what to do. Women raised kids and followed directions. It seems over the years I was great at following directions, never trying to rock the boat.

Now came the source of my biggest regret and a twist that landed me in jail. We got busted on the machines. Yes, there had been a large sting brewing. Joe was tipped off by a police officer who used to drink at our bar, but it was already too late. Federal agents had pictures of the bartenders paying off the customers. The undercover officer had already been in and had all the necessary evidence. Although Joe had taken the machines out the day before the sting operation, it was too late to act dumb since they had the incriminating photos. They raided the bar the next morning as I was pulling into the parking lot.

They didn't want to let me in until I told them I was the actual owner. Entering that bar was a nightmare. The cops had torn everything apart, my kitchen included. In the basement, they found the hot merchandise, which Joe claimed was his but couldn't prove. And one thing you never want to do is fight with the police or act dumb. They did not appreciate me acting surprised about all that. They were not buying the poor-little-wife story, and Joe was acting so cocky. The police told him to sit down. They wanted to talk to only me. I was shaking and very scared. I wasn't prepared for the questions and didn't know how to answer them. I was honest at that point. What else could I do? Lying would only have gotten me in worse trouble.

The bar was a disaster after they got through with it. And they had found something I didn't know existed: Under the bar, Joe had installed mini shelves with guns in them. None of the guns were registered, and all of them were hot. What comes next is not pretty. The license that was displayed behind the bar was in my name, so I was the one taken to jail. Yes, it was the most embarrassing time I've ever experienced in my life. I was still only twenty-six years old, and I was being fingerprinted, having my mug shot taken, and being put in a holding cell until bail could be posted for me. That took hours, and it was not a memory to remember. I was beyond angry and felt totally disgraced in every way. Angry at Joe, angry at myself. How could I get involved with such a thing? Why did I allow it, knowing it was wrong? I guess I was just very submissive and weak.

Once I was released, we immediately retained an attorney. At our first meeting, I learned it was going to cost a fortune. The idea of a "fortune" is all relative to a person's financial status. Ours was not in a place where we could find the money we needed to pay an attorney. We weren't saving money; we spent it as fast as it came in. In my mind, I wanted my kids to have everything I did not have growing up. I got lost in reality. So in the end, we borrowed enough money from Joe's uncle to hire a very good attorney.

Just when you think things are bad and can't get worse, they do get worse. It was maybe six months later when I learned Joe was being followed by the federal agents for suspected car theft—my car, the one I drove my kids around in for two years. My Eldorado was hot. With our son in the car late one afternoon, with it dark outside in the dead of winter, Joe was surrounded by a group of police cars and was picked up on a main road right in front of my sister's beauty school. They handcuffed him and took him straight to jail. My sister was watching from her school and realized it was my car and ran outside to see what was going on. She was informed that my husband was being arrested for possession of a stolen car. My six-year-old son, in the car with my husband, was scared and crying, so my sister was permitted to take him and get in touch with me. I felt like my life was unraveling before my eyes and everything was going downhill.

Joe's brother was trying to post bond to get him out, but the bail was high and it would take a couple of days to get the monies. *Good, let him rot,* I thought. When he finally was released and came home, I told him I wanted a divorce and kicked him out. It was the week of our tenth anniversary and the end of my marriage, for all intents and purposes. No job, no income, and now another arrest. And not having made a house payment in months, we were probably going to lose the house, as well. We were barely getting our utilities paid, and now we were faced with two court hearings. It was certainly not what I wanted for my family. For ten years, I had given the benefit of doubt to my husband so many times. I finally became honest with myself. I always felt I knew he was a cheat; I had just blocked it out. I knew the sketchy business deals going on in the bar were illegal, but I'd just blocked it out. Same for the poker machines and all the hot items being sold out of my garage. I knew deep inside that all of it was wrong, but I was a weak woman and I just played the game of *Hide the Elephant*. I turned the other cheek just to make everyone look at my family and wish they could be us, the perfect family. It was me living the lie, and I take full responsibility for my actions. I was a very dependent and not very confident woman.

My sister Judy moved in to help with the bills, and I got a small job in retail. The kids were in school. I knew the house was going to go into foreclosure, but I couldn't do anything about it. I had just enough for utilities, food, and gas for a junky car I was given to drive. I wanted nothing to do with

Joe. He ended up getting an apartment close by and would take the kids on weekends. He tried everything he could do to get me back, but I stayed firm; there was no way I wanted him back. Judy lived with me for about a year. I knew it would take a long time to foreclose on the house and wasn't even worried about it at the time. I was in survival mode. But that didn't stop Joe from trying to break me down. He wasn't the type of man who took the word "no" very well.

I was in a deep hole and couldn't figure out how to get out of it. I was afraid of the unknown and had the two children crying for their daddy all the time. I look back at that poor, fearful woman and feel very sorry for her. She had led a life so filled with manipulation since childhood that she didn't know how to stand alone on her own two feet.

After close to a year later, Joe knew what buttons to push. He knew how much I loved Florida and how I had never wanted to leave. So he told me he wanted to get back together and move to Florida away from all the past and start over fresh. Hmm. I had been down that road before as a kid, I thought, two different times: once with my real father and once with my stepfather. I knew what it felt like to start bouncing around like a ball. Was I starting to do the same thing to my own kids? What was the alternative?

Divorce? I had seen my mother struggle and get crazy, and I didn't want to be her. So I went and gave it another shot. I did it, the same thing my mother had done; I ran away from my so-called problems, thinking I could start a new life in Florida and that would take away all the memories of my crazy marriage over the last ten years. Then it hit me again—I had become my mother. *Oh no!* I thought.

We packed up all our belongings and gave the house back to the bank. We had less than two thousand dollars in our pocket, two kids, a dog, no house to go to, and no job waiting. We just went, ending up in Bradenton, Florida. I can't believe we were that stupid and took that plunge. Within a couple of days, we found a rental company that let us rent without proof of a job—go figure. Joe managed to get a job at a local convenience market, but we barely made ends meet. We only had one car, so I stayed home, and when the kids would come home from school, we would walk wherever we needed to go. Eventually, Joe found a small dealership, a "buy here/pay here" lot where we could get a cheap beater for me to drive. After that, I could get a job. We were then both working and trying to rebuild our marriage and life. In the back of my head, I knew it was never right or ever going to be right for us. I just existed and was numb. I loved my kids so much I tried to keep us together as a family. That was always my main goal, and at least the kids and I were safe. Joe was never an abusive man, so I wasn't afraid of him. He just couldn't make a living the legal way. He didn't have a formal education, so whenever an opportunity came up that he thought could make money, he took the chance. Also, he liked his ladies and could not stay faithful. *Oh no!* I thought again when I realized I'd not only turned into my mother; I had married a man like my father as well.

We lasted in Florida nine months, a full school year. We arrived just in time for the kids to enroll in school and left Florida in June. How did that happen?

The next phase of my life started when my parents were transferred to Colorado. It was around the same time that we moved to Florida. My stepdad was doing well in his new job after their move, so my parents sent airline tickets so we could spend Christmas with them in Colorado. *Ok,* I thought. *That would be nice.* Little did I know that once we were there my husband would want to move to Colorado. I was bewildered. We had just settled into our home in Florida, I loved Florida, and the kids were happy. I didn't want to leave, but my controlling family sided with Joe and convinced the kids that it would be nice to be around relatives, and they fell for it.

By that time, Joe had a good job with The Coca-Cola Company. As soon as we returned from our trip to Colorado, he put in for a transfer and got it. In June, my parents flew to Florida to help us pack for the road trip to the Centennial State. I cried my eyes out the day they arrived. I wanted to stay in Florida, but I had no choice. Joe was going with the kids and had my parents to back the whole thing up.

How many times must a person start over? I was becoming my mother even more so. I tried so hard to form roots and not move around, but I made the choice the day I married Joe to stick by him for better or worse. Little did I know where that philosophy would lead me.

The drive to Colorado was depressing. We had nowhere to live, so we were going to be staying at my parents' house until we found a place. Great—just the place I wanted to go. Only this time I was grown, married, and had kids, so I guessed I was safe. My mother still had a way of abusing me but just in a different form.

I think we stayed there only for the summer, because before summer was over we had found a house to buy. My parents loaned us the money for a down payment. We got settled in and the kids started school again in a new area. I felt so bad for them. They were living the life I had led; only I was the mother this time. We were moving like crazy people, something I thought I'd left behind in my teen years. That was the one thing I had not wanted to happen.

While Joe went on with his job at Coca-Cola, I eventually got a job, the kids were back in school, and we tried to get back to a normal life again. I guess either you conform or you don't. I tried to accept and make the best of it. We began to make friends with a few of the neighbors, and the kids got involved with sports and were doing well at their new school. We also joined a couples' bowling league and hosted a card night once a month at our house. We did have a beautiful home, so once again I conformed to our new life.

During our time in Colorado, Linda was around eleven years old when she came home from school one day, complaining of pain in her groin. She had been playing a sport outside at school, and I thought maybe she'd pulled a muscle. I put some ice on her and watched for the next couple of days. When her pain did not go away, I took her to a doctor and they ran some tests. The diagnosis was either a hernia or a tumor. So he performed a biopsy, found it was a fatty tumor, removed it, and explained to us that the condition was not uncommon among adolescents. The doctors said it probably would never return. But just two years later, when she was thirteen, Linda started feeling pain in the same area. I took her back to the physician, and he found that the tumor had reoccurred, so it was removed a second time. No follow up was required because the doctor said it just was a fluke, would never come back, and was nothing to worry about as it wasn't cancerous.

Ok, I figured, *the doctors must know what they're doing, and sometimes these things happen.* I felt that with Dr. Parson, her physician, being highly respected in his field, he would surely be on top of it, and we trusted his word.

Meanwhile, as the years went by, Joe came across an opportunity to purchase a pizza restaurant on a land contract. It was a franchise pizza shop, and he found out about it while on his weekly route with Coca-Cola. From what I understood, the owner/franchisor, Gary, wanted to sell that particular location, which was his main restaurant. Joe met with Gary, who presented my husband with a proposal. There was only one catch: Joe was going to keep his job and I was to run the restaurant. When he told me what he was thinking, I immediately said "No!" I knew exactly how owning your own business works—you marry it. I wasn't going to give up my life to run a restaurant. My kids were still young, and I remembered what had happened in the bar business.

Well, we fought about it back and forth for days, maybe weeks. We fought so much even the kids were getting very upset. It was disrupting their lives, and I was not happy. But I eventually broke down. Yes, once again I gave in and quit my job to run a large pizza restaurant that I knew nothing about. I was told by the owner/franchisor that he would train me for three months solid before he turned the restaurant over to us. I wasn't that excited about learning all the aspects of running a pizza restaurant. It was sizable, which meant I had over twenty-five employees to manage when I had never tackled anything like that before. Ultimately, I just accepted the challenge. Joe assured me I wouldn't be working my life away for long—just a year. Then, after that, I would just work part time and things would be easier. So I quit my job that I loved—leasing condos—to become a business owner again. *This time it is going to be different,* I told myself. I was older, more confident, and in charge. And Joe was keeping his day job.

It was an interesting time, to say the least. I think I was in my early thirties at that point. The kids were getting bigger, so I didn't feel as guilty about not being there as soon as they got home from school. I gave it all I had, and it worked out great for the first three months. After firing certain employees who had been stealing the previous owner blind, our profits were amazing. I even got a better handle on the inventory and scheduling. If we could maintain the momentum and keep sales steady, I felt I could see a silver lining. However, Joe got a whiff of greed again and found out that another franchise was selling a few miles away. And it was the same pizza chain, just with a different owner for that store. Of course, Joe wanted it. He wanted to now quit his own day job and run that operation himself. We had made a hefty profit in the three months we had been in business, but I felt we should finish out the first year to see the financial peaks and valleys before jumping into another business. However, my well-intentioned resistance didn't matter any longer. I was a victim of myself. I was weak. I should never have let it happen again, but I did. I guess I still had not formed a backbone yet.

Thus, exactly three months into business with the first restaurant, we bought the second store and Joe did quit his job to run it. I was so afraid there would not be enough money left over to pay our own salaries so we could run our home. Joe said not to worry, it would be fine, and so I believed him. Things got a little tough and tight. We were buying failing businesses and trying to turn them into positive ones, but that was not an easy task to do in a few short months. We worked like dogs seven days a week from sun up to sun down. The kids did homework in the booths at the restaurant, and their daily diet consisted of pizza or pasta. My daughter was now twelve, and my son was only ten. When they were not in school, they were with me at the restaurant, and Linda was even working in the kitchen there.

I noticed there was a karate studio in our plaza, and I asked the owner if he would barter with me. If my son could take lessons, I would in turn feed the studio owner and his employees pizza any time they wanted. That worked out well. It kept my son out of trouble while at the same time allowing me to run the business.

My Unexpected Journey

Ok, here is the straw that broke the camel's back: After three additional months, Joe wanted to buy a third location. That pizza restaurant was twenty-five miles from Denver, but once again I got weak and let it happen. We purchased another one of the failing franchises. Little did I know that that was the beginning of the end of my marriage. For starters, the three businesses were not profiting at all, and to run them, I was stealing from Peter to pay Paul, as the saying goes. I was not able to keep up with the bills on all the businesses and run the large one as a hands-on owner. Our own personal bills were past due, including our house payment. Joe and I had so much stress, and we were fighting nonstop. I got to a point where I just broke. I was exhausted. I was working and killing myself for nothing because, at the end of the day, we were still in a financial hole. I couldn't imagine losing another house. I'd worked so hard that time. I wasn't giving it up. But within four years after that, everything came crashing in on us. Greed had set in once more, and I was there to watch it take us down again.

In hindsight, I would ask, "How stupid could someone be?" I had seen the writing on the wall way before Joe was going to admit it. Now here we were again, in a hole we would never be able to climb out of. The pressure of yet another financial mess and our past problems that we had never really settled came crashing down on me. I wanted out, and there was no more trying. I literally broke. I finally hit my cracking point. Yes, I was now thirty-five, and I had given sixteen of those years to that marriage. I had been through hell and back with that man. I had forgiven all the affairs (somewhat), I'd gotten past the last business failure and the loss of the home in Ohio, but that was it. I would go no further.

I remember one night I was crying at home, folding towels, when my sister, who is six years younger than I, came over and saw me. I had been crying to her since the first mess in Ohio. Well, her words pushed me to the point I never thought I would take. She called me weak, a wimp, and said I was afraid to stand on my own and she would no longer listen to me cry and complain. She had listened to me complain for too many years. She then said she would never try to help me any longer, turned around, and walked out of my house. I hated her at that moment because she had made me look in the mirror and face my demons. Everything she said was the truth. I just was still hiding the *elephant*.

I now said to myself, "I can and will do this." I didn't exactly know how, but I knew I had to get out of that crazy life. After sixteen years of giving all I had to give, I was ready to walk. *And I'll show my sister I am not a wimp or weak—watch me,* I thought.

It's truly amazing that when you are ready to change your life, things just seem to pop up at the right time. By that time, my dad's company had transferred my parents and two sisters back to Ohio. Their huge mountain home in Colorado sat empty, waiting for a buyer. My sister Judy stayed in Colorado, living on her own. She called my mother and told her everything that was going on with me and how she felt I was at my breaking point. After all I had been through in the past with my husband, both my parents were concerned I was going to crack. They despised Joe beyond words. My parents knew the only reason I put up with all of the dysfunction was for my children and trying to keep my family together.

The next day, I was in my basement office, paying some bills and working on invoices, when the phone rang. "Hello," I answered, and the subsequent conversation was very short. It went like this:

"Jackie, this is Mom. How are you and the kids?"

I answered, "We are all just great." I lied.

My mother said, "I just want to let you know that your sister has the keys to the mountain home; it's yours to use any time. Have a nice day."

I hung up the phone and was frozen in the moment. *I am out, I am free, I am leaving him now.* "Thank you, Lord!" I cried.

The same night, Saturday, Joe and I had "The Talk." I told Joe, "I want a divorce, and I can no longer live this life and will not live like this anymore." I knew it was the point of no return. Nothing was ever going to work out with us. I just could not take another day under his thumb. I had to find myself, and that wasn't going to be possible with him around. He thought that it would be just a small separation, that in time I would come to my senses and go back with him. I let him think whatever he wanted, but I knew the truth. I would never go back.

Jackie Dobrosky

When the moving truck came on Monday, the neighbors were surprised. From the outside, we looked like the perfect family with the perfect house, business, cars, kids. No one expected me to move out. You see, I had perfected the *Hide the Elephant* game. But now the game was over. I was out of there. I was actually walking away from my home and I didn't care what the neighbors thought, either. I had fire inside me and nothing was going to stop me. *I'll show my sister I am not a weak wimp. I can do this—and without Joe.*

Joe went as far as helping me move into my parents' large house, which sat along a golf course in the foothills of the Colorado Mountains. Joe and I decided to split the furniture. I was taking the kids to live with me, but he would see them whenever he wanted. It seemed like a dream; everything was so easy and working out smoothly. I was out of the house, and Joe was cooperating. But remember, he didn't think this was permanent, and I just went with it. Why rock the boat? I was in the driver's seat, and it felt empowering. I finally realized I was strong; I could make my own decision.

As we were just getting settled in our new home, my son, then ten years old, was not handling it very well. He could not understand why I was leaving Daddy and the home he had loved. I explained to him that it was just for a short time and that once his dad and I worked out our problems, things would not be like this. We set up his bedroom in the room next to mine. He was always scared at night, and the mountain house being so big—about six thousand square feet—didn't help.

Joey continued to have a hard time living with me in the mountain house. He was still frightened, and he missed his friends. I should have been more understanding of his feelings. Yet I was under so much pressure at that time, and he continued to gripe about living there. He refused to listen and fought with his sister non-stop. I sat him down one afternoon and told him I understood he was not happy but that we had to work together and not fight. He didn't want to hear anything from me. I was trying to appease him, but it wasn't working. He wanted to go live with his father, so I gave him the choice and he chose to go with his dad. I thought he was bluffing, but he never came back.

Whereas the old Jackie would have folded and moved back to keep the family together, the new Jackie had her sister's words buried in her head: "Weak. Wimp. You're just afraid you can't make it on your own." The words kept ringing in my mind, and I drew strength from them. No way was I going to fold again. I would stand firm. *Let him go to his dad's house. I give it a week, and he will be back,* I thought. So he went. I still had my daughter with me, and I would take care of what needed to be taken care of first.

Linda was entering the teen years with a vengeance, and she was a tough cookie. I think we must have bucked heads from the time she realized I was the mother and she was the daughter. Thus, Linda was not exactly the easiest child to raise. In fact, the only person who could control her was her father. I vowed to never raise my hands to my children, and I stood firm on that, so whenever things got too out of hand, I would just call Joe. He never abused her, but he knew how to handle her, and yes, she got her backside smacked many times. But now she was with me and I didn't know what to expect. I just took one day at a time.

Joe and I agreed that through our separation I would run the large restaurant and he would run the other two. That meant no more merging monies from the different locations and no interfering with each other's responsibilities. He would have to be responsible for the two restaurants, and I would have to maintain my own funds to keep my portion of the business running. I held up my end of the agreement easily as I didn't want any part of the other restaurants. Joe, on the other hand, wouldn't stay away from mine. He kept walking in to the restaurant I was running and behaving as if nothing were different. He would act like he was still the boss and even help the crew make pizzas. The guy just didn't get it!

As I stated earlier, Joe was very ego driven. He thought he was going to play along with my game with his own rules. I, however, knew differently. I called him out about his interference many times, but he ignored me. I then met with my managers and explained that they were to work for me; they were being paid by me—not by Joe. I told them that if I came in there and found Joe was in the backroom making pizzas, then it was the two managers who would have to answer for it.

When I repeated to Joe what I had discussed with the managers, he smirked and said, "Okay, Jackie. Whatever."

"Whatever," I thought, was not a correct answer. I knew I had to change my approach. I had to let the whole staff know who was running the show now. I always had weekly meetings every Saturday morning at the restaurant. At the next meeting, I told my staff the new rules. Making myself as clear as I could, I explained everything about my situation with Joe. I fully expressed that I didn't want him in the back kitchens or having anything to do with orders, deposits, or taking food from one restaurant to another. We were no longer together.

But still there were times when I would come in and find Joe out back, talking to the pizza drivers and smoking cigarettes. I was afraid he was bribing them for product, like bags of mozzarella, if his other stores were running short. I had to fire at least a couple of my employees for giving away my inventory because Joe, by appearing so kind and sweet, convinced them he was still part owner of that restaurant. Once again, wrong answer. *This guy just doesn't get it, does he?* I thought again.

One day, Joe took my Ford Bronco and traded it in for a BMW. My ten-year-old son, who was with him, thought that was such a nice thing for his dad to do for me. He didn't understand the mind manipulation; he only saw his great dad trying to make Mom happy and to get back together. I, of course, resented that highly. Living in Colorado, I liked my four-wheel drive. What was I supposed to do with a BMW that was a rear-wheel drive? To make matters even worse, Joe didn't actually buy it for me. He traded in one vehicle for another and then I was sent the payment book. This was so out of line, and his behavior was starting to scare me. Therefore, after about six months into our so-called separation, I retained an attorney. I wanted a divorce.

When Joe received papers saying I had filed for a divorce, I think something snapped in his head. He went crazy. *How could she?* he must have thought. He probably figured our little time out was just me being in a bad mood and as soon as things turned around with the business I would come to my senses and take him back. I always had in the past, so why not now? Well, for starters, I was beginning to get my strength and build up my newfound confidence, and no one was taking it away again. I kept thinking about how much of a victim I had been my entire life, starting with my mother and then moving on to my husband. My sister's words kept resonating in my head: "You're weak. A wimp. You're afraid you can't make it on your own."

Well, I'll show everyone. I can do it and I will do it on my own, I repeated to myself. I wanted my life back, and I kept my focus on that.

Day by day I became stronger. I wasn't going back. I knew it was not going to be easy, but I was willing to take the plunge. I'd had almost thirty-six years of people controlling my life; now it was my turn.

During the months after I filed, my parents sold their mountain home and I had to find a new place to live. *No big deal,* I thought. *I have done this lots of times. I may have even mastered the art of moving.*

I found a condo close to the restaurant, but by that time my daughter had also decided to live with her father. Both kids were very upset with me for filing for divorce from "poor dad." They said their dad was sad, that he didn't want a divorce, that I was the one breaking up the family. Now I will say, years ago his tactic would have made me fold and go back, but it wasn't working any more. I had truly made up my mind. That marriage was over and had been for several years. I hoped someday my kids would understand, but I knew if I didn't leave, I would either die or crack up.

I kept the business running well enough that I could maintain the overhead and even take a paycheck to live off. I was doing okay. I rented a three-bedroom condo and set up a bedroom for each of the kids. Whenever they wanted to come back or visit, I wanted them to feel like they had their own space. As it turned out, Linda came the most. We always had a sort of love/hate relationship. Maybe it's a mother/daughter thing; I'm not sure. But when she missed me, she would come over and stay.

Seven or eight months into the new living arrangements, she caught me off guard one day. While we were watching TV, I brushed her hair as she sat on the floor in front of me and I was on the sofa. Out of the blue, she hit me with a question that shocked me.

"Mom, when are you going to start dating?"

Date? I thought. That hadn't entered my mind.

"Why do you ask such a thing?" I replied.

"Well, Dad has a lot of girlfriends and all you do is work and stay alone," she informed me.

Hmm, I said to myself, *that doesn't surprise me in the least.* I explained that I wasn't ready to date, that I wanted her and her brother back; they were all I needed. She asked me again about dating and sort of called me out by adding, "Are you afraid you can't find another guy besides Dad?"

Okay, that did it. She had just called my bluff. I was on a roll now. I told her, "Give me a couple weeks and I will." I decided I should open my options to find a friend, just a male friend. I worked way too hard. I didn't have time to do anything but run my restaurant. But I would try to begin the process of having at least a meager social life.

Soon I was thinking of going on my first date—but who would have thought it would be with one of the vendors for my restaurant? He had been flirting with me for years, even when I was married, and I had just blown it off. But the next time he came into the restaurant, being his usual cheerful self, I was sitting in a booth, preparing a deposit. I sized him up and thought, *Cute. Blond hair. Blue eyes. Tall. The total opposite of my husband. Not bad. At least he can speak fluent English.* I chuckled. *Not a man I would have thought about till now.*

After he'd finished his work that morning, he came over to me with the invoice. I asked him how he was doing and sort of flirted with him, and his face turned bright red. He hadn't been expecting me to be so playful as I had always been very businesslike with him in the past. He'd always been the playful one. I think I caught him off guard. *Hey, I guess I still got it,* I thought as I smirked to myself. So that day he didn't rush off. Instead, he decided to have lunch at my restaurant, and I treated him to some pizza and joined him. We talked about light subjects, laughed a little bit, and then he left. I sat there after he'd gone and said to myself, *He will be my first date. Where else can I go to meet anyone? All our old friends are married, and it's very true once you get a divorce they seem to disappear. And the fact that I am the one who is divorcing Joe and the one to leave the house, as well as Joe having both kids, doesn't look good for me.*

See? I'd hidden the *elephant* so well that no one had ever suspected anything; everything looked great from the outside. But still, every day I kept the fire alive inside me. I wasn't going back. I knew I could do it.

Things went on as usual for a while, and I continued to see Linda more than Joey. She was now working in the front kitchen at my restaurant on weekends. Because my condo was close to the restaurant, it was easy for her to stay with me then. On the other hand, Joey seemed to put up an emotional block between us and was very cold. I would see him, but there always seemed to be strings attached. For instance, when he needed new tennis shoes or wanted money for something. It was never just to spend time with me. I got that message right away. He didn't want to make his dad feel bad, and by treating me that way it gave his dad power over me. Well, at least that's what he thought. Therefore, I played my cards close to my chest. I knew it was going to be a mind game, and Joe knew the kids were everything to me. But what he didn't know was I was willing to back off and let him be the one they felt sorry for. I'm sure he didn't think I could stand firm.

Jackie Dobrosky

I kept running my restaurant, seeing the kids when I could. I didn't do much besides that. I didn't have any real friends now. As I said, they were all married and busy with their own lives. Occasionally they would come into the restaurant and have pizza with their kids. Other than that, I just worked.

One day while I was putting in a liquor order, six weeks after having pizza with Don, the vendor for my restaurant, he stopped in to the restaurant just to say hello, although he wasn't scheduled to be at my business that day. I guess he'd gotten the word from my employees in the back kitchen that I was getting a divorce. He was back to his playful self. I knew he wanted to ask me out, so I made it easy. I asked him if he knew where I could buy a gun. I told him I wanted to get a permit to carry. I figured because I ran a and regularly carried a lot of cash, I could be a target and I wanted to protect myself. Don was very helpful and offered to take me to a gun shop and then a shooting range to practice.

We met that Saturday afternoon, and we had a great time. He was so kind and helpful as I purchased the gun and then went to the shooting range, where he taught me to shoot. It sounds like a weird first date, but it was fun! He also took me to an early dinner and then brought me back to my restaurant. He was a perfect gentleman. With a smirk on my face, I thought, *I can do this*. It was the beginning of my new life.

As things went along, I started to see Don more frequently but not too often. He had a nine-to-five job Monday through Friday, and our schedules completely conflicted. I worked nights and weekends. In the restaurant business, that's when we make the bulk of our money, so it was like restaurant suicide to go away on the weekend. I was there from open to close on those days. I could maybe get away in the evening during the week on a slow night, but we always made it an early evening because of his job. That was okay, though. I didn't want to get involved too much, anyway.

Everything I did had always remained very private. However, it somehow got back to my husband that I was seeing Don. I don't remember how it got out, but Joe went ballistic. He was a crazy man. He began to stalk me at night, following me after I left the restaurant. I didn't realize it at first. I'd never gone through anything like that before. But when I became aware, I got scared. Joe would park his car outside of my condo and wait—for what or for whom, I don't know. I let Don know about the situation because I was afraid of what Joe might do to him, but Don wasn't intimidated. He knew Joe. In fact, he was the vendor at our other restaurants, also.

I started to think, *Oh my! This may have been a bad idea. It's just too close. I should have never involved Don in this craziness.*

Even though Joe had been dating multiple women and bringing them around my kids, I had stayed quiet and kept my relationship with Don under wraps for the sake of the kids. And then Joe turned around and told my kids I had a boyfriend and that I had probably left the marriage because of Don.

After that, it got real crazy. I thought Joe had flipped. He was certainly on the war path. I don't think even the businesses mattered to him then; he was determined to get me back. He went as far as to fly to Ohio and get my grandmother, aunts, and cousins involved. (He wouldn't have gone to my parents; they hated him.) He worked on the weak links first. He cried to everyone who would listen, thinking they would change my mind and convince me to go back with him. *No way,* I thought. *I would die first.* I was finally out of his grips and intended to stay that way. No phone calls from Ohio had any effect on me. I wasn't about to live with someone just because they said so. I had given that man sixteen years, and it was over. But the more I stood my ground, the harder it became. It got to the point where even the kids were being used just to reel me back to Joe. No, I was firm. I wanted a divorce. I had put up with enough. It was over.

Christmas was approaching soon, and it was a tough year in our family, not only due to my divorce. We had also lost my grandfather in October and my brother's wife in November. So my mother, stepfather, sister, and brother packed up their van and drove out to spend Christmas with my sister Judy and me. They were going to stay at my condo since I had three bedrooms. I was so hoping for a quiet holiday, but what happened next is unbelievable.

My Unexpected Journey

My family had just arrived in Colorado when Joe pulled his stupidest move of all. He called me on the phone and said he was going to kill himself. I had the kids with me by then, so I figured he was alone in the house, and I told him I would call 911 and have them bust the door down. He hung up on me, and I did call 911 and told the operator exactly what Joe had threatened. My whole family jumped into my dad's van and we drove to the house.

The house—the one I had moved out of and that Joe was still living in—was in a development with a homeowners' association, and there were only two entrances to the community. The police blocked off both entrances to prevent Joe from leaving. But when the emergency crew did actually break the door down, they found out Joe wasn't even in the house.

Joe was a crazy guy with a gun, and we had no idea where he was. *Oh my God, this is not what I need right now!*

Jackie Dobrosky

My family was devastated, to say the least. The kids were crying, and I was so angry Joe would stoop so low, especially at Christmas. After a few hours of trying to find him, we left and went back to my condo. Everyone was so drained, the kids were still crying, and we all decided to just hold hands and pray. Then my stepdad suggested we should pack up the van, take all our Christmas food, and go to a cabin in the mountains. So that's what we did. We had a very nice time and the kids had fun during that holiday week at the cabin. We rented snowmobiles, sleds, and tubes to use on the snow-capped mountain. And even though the heat went out one night while we all slept—and we felt like we were going to freeze—it was still a wonderful memory after all.

Later, we learned where Joe had been the whole time everyone was searching for him. He had not even tried to leave the housing development. Instead, he had snuck out through the back door, gone to the neighbor's house, and was having a beer with Jim, the neighbor, who didn't even know what was going on outside.

After the first of the year, I was getting anxious to get the divorce over once and for all, but we just couldn't agree on the terms. Joe wanted full custody of the kids, and I was not willing to go along with that. He wasn't being fair on the settlement of the businesses, either, and it seemed like he held the gold coin, or so he thought. It had been nearly a year of going through that craziness. I just wanted to put it to rest.

The standoff went on most of the first five months of the new year, and then we had another one of our meetings with the attorneys, but it seemed like we were still hitting walls. I took my attorney out in the hallway and asked why it was taking so long. She explained that with the amount of assets we had, if we couldn't come up with a fair settlement regarding the interests of both parties, it could take another year or so. I just wanted out.

"What is it going to take to get this finished?" I asked her. She replied that short of giving it all away, I would have to have patience and it would take time. Out of that statement, all I heard was "short of giving it all away..."

"How long if I give it all up?" I asked her. Well, she said she didn't think that was the brightest idea in the world; however, she said it could be forty-five days if I walked away with nothing. I told her to tell my husband I wanted nothing, just my freedom.

With that said, we walked back into the room where both Joe and his attorney were sitting. Dottie White, my attorney, addressed Joe's attorney and said we had come up with a settlement that would be acceptable to both parties: "My client wants nothing from the marriage. She relinquishes everything to her husband. All she wants is the divorce and her maiden name back."

If I could have frozen that moment in time, it would be priceless today. There was nothing to fight about, nothing at all. I had thrown the final trump card down.

It ended up taking another two months to finalize the deal. Joe wanted my restaurant back immediately, but I wouldn't agree. I needed to figure out what I was going to do. It appeared I was going back to Ohio, but I needed time. He wanted it right then; it was during the time of year the business was generating a lot of cash, and he needed that extra cash to run his other businesses.

Still feeling strong and a little cocky, I said, "Let's make a deal." His ears perked up at that—he was a master when it came to making deals. "I will turn over the big restaurant to you if you give me custody of Linda to take her back to Ohio." He would have to make the choice between parenting and money. He didn't answer, but I let it go. I knew in my heart he was drowning in debt, so I played it off as if it was no big deal. Take it or leave it. I was still going to run my business for the next two months, make some profits, and then move. He was stuck between a rock and a hard place. One thing I know about Joe: money motivates him and lack of it makes him crazy. So being he was close to craziness already, I knew the outcome would be on my side.

I had already contacted my attorney to have all the information typed up in a letter to make it legal. I was prepared, and I knew I must get Linda back to Ohio. She was hanging out with a bad crowd of friends and doing poorly in school. Acting more like our children's friend than their parent, Joe let the kids do whatever they wanted. Joey was too young to understand that, but Linda was starting to take advantage of her newfound freedom. She needed her wings clipped somewhat.

It was exactly two days later that I got the call from Joe. He said he would sign anything I needed if he could take possession of the business in a couple of days. I smiled. I had finally figured out how to fight like a lady and win!

After a meeting with the attorneys to sign the final documents, with me walking away with nothing but the shirt on my back, so to speak, I went to a liquor store, bought a bottle of vodka, went home, and drew a hot bath. I took my bottle and a glass with me. My way of chilling out. I had just given away everything, including one of my kids. But it helped to know I would get Linda right away. With Joey, however, it was going to take time. He had a bond with his dad I couldn't break.

In the next couple of days, I met with Joe at a bank and had all the paperwork in hand, to be signed and notarized, that would allow me to take Linda back to Ohio. I even had a plane ticket for her to follow me in two weeks. My attorney had advised me on the verbiage of the letter and assured me if I had it notarized it would be a legal contract and binding in a court of law. We went into the bank, signed, and had the document notarized. As I walked away, we each had a notarized copy because I had made two originals. I kissed the kids goodbye, and then I handed Joe the plane ticket for Linda to meet me in Ohio in two weeks. She was not happy, but that was okay. She would get over it, and I knew I had to get her out of Denver before she got herself in trouble. *She might not understand today,* I thought, *but she will someday.* My son was evasive and would not look at me, but I kissed him anyway and told him I would see him soon.

In the following days, I packed up my house and I accepted Don's offer to drive the truck back to Ohio for me. I had said goodbye to my kids, to my business, and to the life I had lived in Colorado. Off I went on my new venture and a new chapter of my life. I was now a free woman, free to live the way I wanted.

CHAPTER 3

The three-day drive back to Ohio was filled with so many emotions. As I was sitting and looking out the window, I was thinking so much about my life and asking myself how I had landed in such a position. I'd just divorced my husband and left the life I'd had for the last sixteen years. I'd left the business I'd worked so hard on for the last four years. I'd left the home I had shared with my kids. I'd just left my kids with their father, and now I was traveling across the country with a man I'd just met six months earlier. Had I gone crazy?

Jackie Dobrosky

I didn't feel crazy. I felt damn good. I knew in my heart that if I hadn't left, I wouldn't have lived. I had been that unhappy. I was willing to give it all up for my freedom. Stuff can always be replaced. Happiness, on the other hand, cannot. Life is way too short to live it miserably.

When we pulled into a gas station to fill the truck up, and I began to walk to the ladies' room, I looked back and saw the truck holding everything I owned. Thirty-six years of my life all fit into a sixteen-foot truck. *How sad,* I thought, and I wondered, *What lies ahead for me?* I didn't know what to expect or what I was going to do, but my new journey had begun. I just prayed and asked God for His help.

After the third day on the road, I was getting very antsy and cranky. I think Don was my angel. He was a gem. As I cried, he had so much patience with me, reassuring me that things were just as they were supposed to be and everything was going to work out just fine. I wanted to believe him, but I was too emotional to care. All I felt was failure. The one thing I had never wanted to fail at was my marriage—I'd really thought it was for life. Then a thought came into my head: Linda would be coming in two weeks. She would have enough time to get settled and would go to school with my sister, as they were only one year apart. Okay. There was my silver lining.

Once we reached Ohio, I got a nervous stomach. What would the people say? What would my family think of me just leaving and moving back to Ohio? Would I be judged for getting a divorce? I came from a small town where people talked. I was always a people pleaser, to a fault. I worried about what everyone thought. How crazy is that? But that was me, and now I worried I'd be condemned for my failed marriage.

No, Jackie. Straighten up! I chided myself. *Who cares anyway?*

I moved in with my parents, putting most of my things in storage for the time being. Don stayed a few days before going back to Colorado, and I knew I would never see him again. He was just my angel to help me get back to Ohio. I will never forget him. He was a kind, patient man who asked for nothing in return. He only wanted to see me happy.

For the next two weeks, I was in total depression, not even wanting to get out of bed. In fact, I don't think I did. Then one day, my Aunt Margie came to visit me at my mother's house. She had always been my favorite aunt, and she convinced me to get out of bed by telling me what I did was not wrong; living like I did for all the wrong reasons and for all those years, that was something else. But getting out was not a cop out. "You tried for too many years," she told me. I thought long and hard about what she said and then got up and took a shower. After that, I didn't look back. I had made my decision, and now I was staying firm and not feeling ashamed. I'd done nothing wrong. Yes, I was broke and somewhat homeless, I felt, and I had no job. But that was just temporary. I still had my own life to live, and I would get the rest back; I was banking on it.

My stepdad sat me down one Saturday morning and we had a talk about a few important subjects, the most important one being my finances. He didn't think I had made the right decision in giving Joe everything and walking away. Just because I gave him everything did not mean I was off the hook, my stepdad informed me. I had signed on all the businesses, and the house was in both names. If Joe failed to make payments on anything, the collectors would be coming after me as well. The only solution was for me to file bankruptcy, he said. I heard him talking, but I felt like I was having an out-of-body experience. How could I add another thing to my already long list of failures? But as my dad explained, I had to cover myself or I would be in hot water, so I set an appointment up with my dad's attorney.

The second thing he wanted to talk about was what I planned on doing with my life now. At thirty-six years old, it would be a long shot to try and get a four-year degree. And by the time I would graduate, I would be too old to begin a new career. I would be competing with younger people for available positions. I asked what he thought I should do, and he answered, "Real estate."

"But don't those people work only on commission?" I asked.

He said, "Yes, but they don't have a ceiling on how much they can make, so it's a win."

I stared at him, dumbfounded. I had to sleep on that one. Tomorrow was another day. I would deal with it then.

My Unexpected Journey

In the meantime, I got a call from my son, informing me that he and his father would be moving back to Ohio. *Oh no, really?* It was a bittersweet call: on one hand, my son would be in the same state with me; on the other hand, I didn't want Joe to stalk me or use the kids as bait. Hadn't everyone been through enough? I never asked about the house, the cars, or the businesses. I was going bankrupt anyway. I was not part of that life anymore.

I thought about the real estate idea the whole weekend. It stood out in my mind that I would be working on my own, for myself, in a new business without much overhead. *Okay, I am ready for this. Let's get started,* I thought. I had never been afraid of starting over. In fact, I think I had mastered it. So I decided to sign up for classes nearby and become a realtor. By then, Linda had arrived from Colorado, and I was getting her ready to start the new school year. She was happy to be going to school with my sister, her aunt.

    I enrolled in real estate school and was studying every night. It was a crash course, only lasting for one month, and I hadn't studied like that in years. I found it very challenging to retain all the information. After completing the class, I took the state test and was fortunate to pass on my first try. I was determined to be the best I could in my new profession. I went out right away, found a broker, set up my desk, and started to get into selling houses. It was a fresh, new start.

CHAPTER 4

It was only a month into my new career that another twist in my journey was about to take place. While eating dinner one night with our family, Linda confessed she was having more pain in her leg. I asked her how long it had been going on. "A couple of months," she replied. She had mentioned it to her father, but he'd just fluffed it off as growing pains. The pain was in the same area where she'd had the past two surgeries. No longer in Colorado, I needed to find a new doctor in our area.

I took her to a family doctor first and explained Linda's past history with tumors in the same area, and she was checked. The doctor told us it was probably scar tissue after they did an x-ray and nothing showed up. So we went home and I vowed to keep an eye on her.

Linda continued at school and attended a formal dance—before everything changed. I remember it like it was yesterday. She wore her first pair of high heels and a blue velvet dress with a slit up the side. She was a new young lady since she had left her so-called "gang" life in Colorado. I was so glad I could get her out of Colorado and away from the group she had been hanging out with there. Little did I know that would be the first and last dance Linda would ever attend.

As the weeks passed, Linda continued to complain. I then took her to another doctor, with the same results. More weeks of waiting, more pain, and three more doctors later, the last one finally ordered an MRI and found her problem: a large tumor in the groin, the same area in which her first tumor had appeared. The doctor was very concerned and set an appointment for us to meet with a specialist at the Cleveland Clinic the following day. To Dr. Joyce, the specialist, I hand-delivered reports and the x-rays taken the day before. After looking at the information, he confirmed the worst news I had ever heard: "She has a tumor that looks like the size of a small football in her groin. It will have to be removed, and it may cause a small change in the way she walks based on its location, but she will still walk."

Good and bad news all at one time. I was having a hard time processing it. "When do you want to do the surgery?" I asked.

Dr. Joyce replied, "Immediately."

When they checked out an available time for the surgery, we were about a week out. The drive back to my parents' house was a blur. How was I going to get through this? I had just gone through a major change in the last two months. I had just gotten my real estate license. Linda had just started school. *Why, God? Why now?* I felt myself falling apart inside. Linda and I never said a word all the way home. I couldn't talk and didn't want to face it. *God hates me. Why my daughter? If He is mad at me for getting a divorce, why take it out on my poor daughter?*

The next day, while at work, I received a call from someone wanting to see a house. I did not own a car yet, so I borrowed my parents' van to show the house. On the way to the showing, I stopped at the gas station and happened to run into a friend I hadn't seen in a long time. She asked if I wanted to grab a drink after I showed the house. I figured, *Why not?* We planned to meet up at a local bar in an hour. We had so much catching up to do as I had been away from the area for years. I met her about an hour later, and the more we talked, catching up on old times, the more I drank. I think the wine was killing the pain in my heart. I never thought for an instant that I maybe should eat something because I hadn't eaten all day, or maybe slow down on the drinks, or just stop drinking. I didn't care. I was numb, and I liked that feeling.

After a few hours, we parted ways, and I should never have driven myself home. For starters, I went the wrong direction on the freeway. And the evening ended with me hitting a tree as I came off a ramp, totaling my parents' van. Great. *Good job, Jackie.* All I remember is being taken in an ambulance to the first hospital. And yes, they did a breath and blood test and I was over the legal limits. I had a big black eye along with two injured knees that needed stitches. I shouldn't have been so surprised. I had downed the drinks like they were Kool-Aid and hadn't had any dinner. What was I thinking?

Jackie Dobrosky

Someone called my parents to come pick me up, and for the first time in thirty-six years, I felt like a ten-year-old getting disciplined. My dad completely lost it, and my mother was screaming. I had a daughter going to the hospital in a week, and there I was, out drinking like a drunken sailor and not thinking about what I should have been doing and preparing for major surgery. I think it was the first time I just didn't care what happened to me. *What could possibly happen worse than this?* I had hit rock bottom. I'd lost my marriage, my businesses, my son, my life as I knew it—and now my daughter was facing a surgery that could change her life forever. I wanted to die, and I had done a pretty good job at trying, but somehow I'd walked away with only minor injuries. How low could I go?

The week before Linda's surgery flew by. I was in pain with the stitches and bruises, and I had to wear makeup to cover my black eye. Linda was upset with me, too. She felt I didn't care about her or I would not have been so irresponsible. She was right. I wanted to run from my problems; it felt easier. But I learned a very important lesson that night. Copping out does not solve any problems. I had to remain clear-headed and think straight. I apologized to everyone, especially my daughter.

The day of her pre-op was Wednesday, just one day away. I knew Linda was frightened, and so was I. The day after pre-op was her check-in date for the surgery. I had packed a suitcase and was going to stay with her in the hospital. I had already called my broker at the office and told her my situation, informing her that I had to take time off. I didn't know how long we were going to be at the hospital, but I wasn't leaving till Linda was released. Little did I know this twist to my life's journey would be the biggest one of all.

Jackie Dobrosky

After we checked in and got comfortable with our surroundings, Linda and I watched a movie and ate dinner together. Her surgery was scheduled for early in the morning, so we went to sleep early as well. The next day came quickly. My parents had made it up to the hospital in time to see her off, and even her father was there. We all held hands, kissed her, said a prayer with her, then off she went. Her surgery lasted at least sixteen hours. We were all nervous wrecks. We had so many people praying for her.

On the morning of the surgery, I couldn't speak, I couldn't even feel myself breathe or drink water; I was so numb. They had three different surgeons in on my case. First, the orthopedic surgeon, then the vascular surgeon, and finally the plastic surgeon. They kept changing shifts and giving us hourly updates. It must have been serious, because the hospital sent a priest to pray with our family and give us support.

After what seemed like an eternity, the surgery was completely finished. The results were not the same as what the orthopedic doctor thought he was getting into. They had run into many more complications than they had anticipated. First, the tumor was located in the deep part of her groin and was much larger than even he had thought. And because it had come back three times, he was very careful to take large, clear margins around the tumor so not to leave any parts or fragments of the monster tumor, especially since it had a lot of veins and roots around it.

The procedure itself had been more complicated than they originally thought, as well. The tumor, a type known as a *desmoid tumor* or *aggressive fibromatosis*, had cut off the femoral artery that supplied blood to the rest of the leg. With the tumor removed from Linda's groin, they had to fill up the cavity with a stomach muscle. In turn, it became very complicated. Now with that being said, we had to wait and see how things were going to turn out. They could not guarantee the leg was not going to have more problems.

As the days went by following the surgery, the foot was becoming cold and turning blue—a bad sign. But at first, the doctors thought they could save the leg that started dying right after they removed the tumor, which had strangled her femoral artery, which in turn was killing her foot. A few days after the surgery and when they were getting very concerned about the wound's progress, they performed a procedure called a fasciotomy to help save the leg by opening the side of the leg and cutting through the fascia to let the blood flow through to the foot. But that did not work. After about a week, it became more than apparent they were not going to be able to save the leg. However, we kept waiting and praying that maybe by some grace of God and a miracle the procedure would work.

Days turned into weeks. We had checked into the Cleveland Clinic in September, and now it was going into November with no apparent change in Linda's condition. She appeared to be as stable as could be expected.

I will never forget one special, spiritual night during that time. It was November thirteenth, just a regular day of our normal routine at the hospital. I had been sleeping in Linda's room on a little cot for months. Every morning after the nurses took Linda's vitals and administered her medications, I sponged her down, changed her pajamas, and brushed her hair. Then I would go down the hall to shower and get dressed for the day. I would sit next to her bedside and watch TV with her or read a book. Linda normally didn't talk much—she was in so much pain every day—but on that particular day, she was quite cheerful. Nothing had really improved, but at the same time, nothing had gotten worse, so that was good. She ate a little, slept a lot, and watched TV.

Later that day, her father came to the hospital to see her. At about ten p.m., I told him I was going to go outside and get some air. Once outdoors, I found a stoop to sit on and just read my book. It was a cold, brisk night, and it felt good to breathe in some fresh air. I was thankful a security guard stood right inside the glass door and could keep an eye on me. The Cleveland Clinic is not in the best of areas. In fact, we generally parked our cars in a secure, gated parking lot at the Ronald McDonald House and then took a shuttle back and forth for the few blocks to the Clinic.

The Ronald McDonald House Charities is an amazing organization that provides a place for parents or other family members to stay close by while a child is hospitalized. One of more than three hundred Ronald McDonald Houses nationwide, the Ronald McDonald House

My Unexpected Journey

(RMH) located near the Cleveland Clinic offers a private hotel room along with smaller rooms for reading, meditating, or spending time alone just to regroup. The RMH has a TV room, game room, and a full kitchen families can use if they choose to bring their own food and cook even though the facility offers frozen dinners, beverages, and cookies for free. There is only a minimal charge per day (seven dollars at the time we stayed there) for as long as you need it. Today, I still donate money to the organization every chance I get in the hopes that these services will continue to be available for families who need them.

But on that night as I sat outside the Clinic, engrossed in my book, a car suddenly pulled up in the horseshoe driveway. When the window lowered, I saw the driver was my mother. *What?* I thought. *How can she be here? She has a hard enough time driving during the day let alone driving an hour and a half from home at night.*

Jackie Dobrosky

I was beyond shocked at the coincidence; but then, I didn't believe in coincidences. My mother had shown up at the exact time I was at that exact spot, so how could it be a coincidence? The Cleveland Clinic is enormous, and there are many different entrances/exits located throughout the facility, and I was sitting outside at that particular entrance at ten o'clock at night.

My mother said, "Jump in." Dumbfounded, I just did what she said before asking her why she was there. "I was washing dishes when something told me I needed to come here, so I packed a bag and jumped in the car," she added.

As we drove to the RMH to drop off her car and put her bag in the room, she kept asking how Linda was doing. I explained that it had been a great day, that she seemed in much better spirits, and that they had been able to get her pain at an acceptable level for her to handle. By the time my mother and I got back to the hospital, though, Linda was fast asleep and Joe was gone. Since the day had gone so well and Linda was resting peacefully, the nurse suggested I go back to Ronald McDonald House, take a hot shower, and get a full night's sleep. That sounded so good to me! Sleeping on the cot had not only been killing my back, it had also brought back memories of sleeping in Grandma's basement as a child. So I decided to follow the nurse's advice but asked her to please call me if anything came up. She promised me she would.

Mom and I waited for the next shuttle and got back to our room. It was amazing how good a hot shower felt. I put on my pajamas, jumped in bed, and then we were both asleep before midnight. At approximately one a.m., the phone rang in our room. I jumped immediately to answer, and it was the hospital. The nurse said Linda had just blown a vein in her leg and it was serious. She informed me that they had a police officer waiting outside the RMH to take us to the hospital. We ran around the room to find our clothes and shoes, which I think took no more than five minutes. The police car was right outside. We jumped in, and they rushed to get us over to the hospital.

As I walked into Linda's room, I wasn't sure what to expect, but what I saw was totally overwhelming. Blankets had been laid on the floor to cover the blood while two nurses administered blood to both arms. A doctor was using the paddle on Linda because her blood pressure was dropping too fast and they were losing her. I was up against a wall—literally up against a wall—and when I looked over, my mother was up against the same wall and could not move. It felt like something very spiritual was happening, like God's angels had their hands on both my mother and me, holding us up so we wouldn't fall.

Linda looked at me with a look I'd never seen before, and the only thing she said to me was, "Mom, am I dying?" I knew she was starting to die; I felt it. But my only words to her were, "Linda, fight! Fight so hard and pray to God. Don't give up!"

Then she was rushed out of the room and into emergency surgery. As my mother and I stood there up against that wall, still holding hands, I looked over at her and I felt like a large angel was in our room, still holding us up against the wall. Like two beautiful hands had just been supporting us in our time of need. I believe that truly. When we finally decided to walk out of the room a few minutes later, I felt such a peace inside me. I knew God was with us. He had sent my mother that night so I wasn't alone when that happened.

It was really a "Footprints in the Sand" moment. God never left my side. He used my mother to be there for me, and I know there was an angel there in the room that night. If not, we would have collapsed, but we didn't. God had us in His hands.

I looked at my mother and said, "You know, Mother, God told you to come here so I would not be alone. He used you to support me in this time. Do you realize that?" And tears filled our eyes.

Even after everything the doctors tried, it was too late to save Linda's leg. It was either her leg or her life. I understand that God does not make bad things happen to people, but I was so upset when I heard the news that I lost it for a while. He brought my mother to be with me on that horrific night so I would not be alone, and now Linda was in surgery and the doctors had just come out to tell me there was no hope and they had to amputate the leg or lose my daughter.

As a mother, it was the most difficult decision I'd ever had to make. She was only fifteen at the time, turning sixteen November twenty-fourth. I died a million times in those hours. "Why, God, why?" I kept asking. Again I thought, *She is just still so young, just beginning her life.* And then, *It's not fair for her to have to lose her leg!* But at the same time, I didn't want to lose my daughter. My emotions were running deep. I wanted to pray, but I couldn't. I was angry. I guess I was angry with God. I didn't realize it wasn't God who was causing her suffering, and I needed someone to blame; I had beaten myself up so much by then that I needed someone I could attack. But my inner self set me straight. It wasn't God's fault. He didn't hate her or me. In fact, although I couldn't have known it at the time, He was to bestow wonderful blessings upon her years later.

I was so lucky my mother was with me that night. Linda's surgery that time was even longer than the sixteen hours the previous one had lasted. Once again, the specialists each took their own shifts as the surgery was performed.

I sat there in numbness for hours. In my mind, I kept going through all the years of surgeries, wondering why the doctors had not been able to find her tumor sooner, before it had gotten so large that it cut off her circulation. I wondered what caused the disease. I had been so careful during my pregnancy, yet I was afraid I had caused it somehow. I was beating myself up so much I almost didn't hear the doctor calling for me.

I snapped back into reality and ran to him.

"How is she? Is she going to live?" I demanded.

He said he felt hopeful, but now it was just an hour-by-hour thing we had to wait through. Once again, three surgeons—orthopedic, vascular, and plastic—were taking shifts. We had no choice but to just go back into the waiting room. We also contacted family members to let them know what was happening.

The surgeons came out to talk to us between the changing of the specialists. Even worse than her last surgery, this was a live-or-die situation. I knew they were amputating the leg. Once gangrene sets in, there is no hope, especially in Linda's situation.

Please, God, don't let her die. She's only fifteen.

I'd never felt so numb. I felt as if I still couldn't even breathe or drink water. *How can this be happening? Why didn't they detect this months before? What happened? Who dropped the ball?* I had to blame someone. I was carrying around so much guilt. *Please let me wake out of this nightmare,* I prayed.

It must have been late in the afternoon when a staff member told us Linda was in recovery. Sixteen-plus hours and three doctors later, she was finally in recovery. I couldn't wait to see her, but I was also afraid to see her. I didn't know how I would react. *God,* I prayed, *don't leave me. Keep me strong.* At that point, I had a love/hate relationship with God. I was angry, but I needed Him. When we were allowed in the recovery room, Joe and I went in first. Linda had her eyes only groggily open, but she knew both of us.

There was an empty look on her face, and the first thing she said was, "Did they take my leg off?"

"Yes, honey, they had no other choice," I replied. Then she turned her head away from me and closed her eyes. I wanted to puke. I felt like I was going to pass out. *I can't do this.* Joe didn't say much, and neither did I. At that point, the only thing we had in common was our two children.

My family ended up staying overnight at the RMH. When Linda came out of recovery, they put her in the Intensive Care Unit (ICU) for the night, so I went to the

RMH also, but I had no idea how I was going to get to sleep. I was just a walking zombie. Back at the house, I sat alone in one of the living rooms. I didn't want to be around anyone. I couldn't talk. I had to process the whole nightmare. *Will I ever come to grips with what just happened? How did she get this tumor disease? Did I do something wrong in my pregnancy?* I wondered again and again. I was so guilt ridden. *God, please let her be okay.*

Very early the next morning, I went back to the hospital. The nurses said Linda had had a peaceful night and they were moving her out of the ICU to another room. She was now stable for the time being. As I collected my belongings out of her old room to bring to the new one, I decided I was not leaving the hospital. No matter how long it took, I had to watch her.

The next couple of weeks were so hard. Linda cried a lot, and I cried a lot but never in front of her. She always said I was hard as nails. Little did she know that as soon as I was out of her sight I lost it, but I had to be strong in front of her; I am her mother.

It was nearing the end of November, and Linda spent her sixteenth birthday in the hospital. We got her a cake and sang to her. Linda had a private room and she needed every inch of it—we had so many flowers, plants, stuffed animals…you name it, they were coming in by the handfuls. Cards were displayed on a cork board for her to look at, and my sister Christine painted the image of a large fish tank on Linda's window. It took her days to complete it, but the end result was amazing. It took up the whole window. When you entered Linda's room, you had to get happy; you had no choice. It was like something from Disney World. People would pass in the hallways just to peek in. I know that made Linda happy and showed her that people loved her, that her family loved her, but she was so angry with God.

She blamed Him for everything, and she blamed me for not finding the problem sooner. That broke my heart, because I did try, over and over. But the doctors kept missing the problem. They were not used to treating such a very rare tumor disease.

One day not too long after Linda's surgery, we noticed a spot on her stomach that was getting red. Her staples had not been removed yet, but somehow she had contracted a staph infection. Soon, the doctor came in and had to remove the staples in a certain area and drain out the pus. I stood right there and helped the doctor and nurses as they opened her wound and cleaned out the area of infection. What I never thought I could do, I did for my daughter. I asked God to give me strength, and boy, did He give it to me.

With the staples out and the pus drained, they packed the incision so it would heal from the inside out. It was a massive, wide-open cavity. A few days later, the infection got worse and set into her bloodstream. She spiked a fever of one hundred six degrees. Her doctor came back in and put her whole body on an ice sheet, and she had to lie on it till her fever broke.

Every time we thought she was getting close to being released, something else showed up. After the amputation, she had other infections set in, and many more surgeries took place before the doctor let her come home. She had been admitted into the Cleveland Clinic in mid-September and didn't leave until mid-December, getting home just in time for Christmas. After leaving the hospital, we went back to my parents' house. My parents were more than gracious to us. The hospital ordered all types of medical equipment and a hospital bed that we put in my parents' family room because, in their two-story house, we could not get Linda upstairs to a bedroom. My dad even had a ramp built for her in the garage so we could get into the house more easily.

The hospital scheduled nurses to visit two times a day to change the dressing on Linda's leg and repack the incision from the staph infection. Over the months, I also learned how to do the dressing changes, so that cut down on some of the nurses' visits.

I don't know what I would have done without my parents and family during those times. I never left Linda's side, so I was not working at the time. My only goal was to help my daughter get better. I was broke, had no home of my own, and had a very sick daughter—and besides that, Linda's father would not even help out. Financially, he never gave a dollar, not one. Oh, he would visit, but he would not give any money to help take care of his daughter. I knew someday he would pay the price through his own Karma; I didn't have to do a thing.

As time went on, Linda got a tutor from her high school to teach her at home and I found a new company to place my real estate license with. My previous broker was not happy I had taken so much time off to take care of my daughter, and I decided that was not a company I wanted to work for, so I moved on. I could get out a few days a week to work. I wanted to make some money so I could move out on our own. I was in a real predicament. Joe never offered to give me a penny, not one stinking penny, while Linda was sick. He was going to make my life miserable, I guess. I'm sure he thought he was getting back at me by not helping with his only daughter. I took it with a grain of salt, however. *I'll do this alone,* I swore to myself. *When the time is right, I will be back on my feet.*

Meanwhile, Grandma Ann, my stepdad's mom, was getting up there in age and could no longer live on her own, so my parents decided to move her to an assisted-living facility. The first thing that came to my mind was, *Can Linda and I take over the lease?* The rent was four hundred twenty-five dollars per month. Linda was now getting Social Security Income of six hundred fifty dollars per month, and I was certain I would soon be making enough money that we could handle the costs. Once again, my dad sat me down and told me that I didn't have to move out. My response to that was, "Yes, Dad, I do. I need my dignity back." He reiterated that we didn't have to leave, but in the end, he understood where my values were, and I think he respected that in me.

So the first of the following month after Grandma moved out, I rented a U-Haul and went to the storage area to retrieve my possessions. You would think we were moving into a mansion, we were so happy. I didn't have much, grant you, but I had enough. We put our little place together, and it was darling—small, but all ours. I was working hard at my job, but in real estate, it takes time to build your business, and I just didn't have the means to wait. I decided to find income by supplementing with other jobs. I put an ad in the paper to find work as a housekeeper. In no time, I had filled my desired five days per week. In the afternoons, then, I worked real estate. But that still wasn't enough money, so I applied for a job at a nursing home, working eleven p.m. to seven a.m., five days a week, but sometimes I worked on weekends. You see, I had to have a flexible schedule because I had to take Linda to the Cleveland Clinic at least two to three times per week, so I worked my other jobs around that.

I worked day and night that first year on top of taking care of my daughter alone. God was giving me great help, I know. I worked for everything we had—and it wasn't much, but what Linda and I had now was priceless: our own place. I could get a car now, and my dad co-signed for me. There was enough coming in to pay for my car, rent, utilities, and food. Linda did receive food stamps, and it was very hard for me to accept them, but I never used them for more than six months. For me, it was not a lifestyle; it was a stepping stone. I stayed very positive. I would not let anyone tell me I could not make it or could not survive. I did it on my own, and I am not ashamed of what I was able to accomplish. It was what I called picking myself up and getting back into the game of life. I never looked back—why should I? Looking back only stops the process of growing to new levels.

Life went by quickly then, it seemed. I was just blessed that Linda was getting stronger, and by the time three months had passed, she was ready to start considering a prosthetic leg. She was happy yet scared about wearing one. I already was taking her to the Cleveland Clinic so much my car could drive there by itself. And now it was another visit to the doctor, this time to make the prosthetic leg. I must tell you, during one of the surgical procedures, the doctors had removed major muscles in Linda's thigh, her flexors and abductors in the hip. Because she was now lacking these important muscles, it would be much more difficult—but not impossible—for her to move her leg when she walked. But the first prosthetist we consulted told my daughter, who was just sixteen and had just lost her leg, it would be impossible for her to ever walk. Therefore, I took that gentleman out into the hallway and asked him not to come back and to send me someone else. No one was going to tell Linda she couldn't do it before she even tried. I just wouldn't accept it.

The prosthetist continued to press the issue by saying, "Mother, you are in denial. She will never walk."

I said, "You're fired off this case. Bring me someone with a more positive attitude." (Boy, did that feel good. I don't work well with negative people.) Then I went back into the room, and when Linda looked at me with the look as if she knew what I had done, I just smiled. Every day I was getting better at saying "No." *No* is a healthy word. I use it frequently when it's needed.

For almost an hour, we sat in that room after I had dismissed the prosthetist, and Linda was angry with me. She thought no one was going to work with us because I was difficult. On the other hand, I felt that the right one would walk in the door. I had plenty of time that day, so we would just wait it out. Soon, a nice young gentleman very cautiously entered the room. I think he was wary; who knows what that other guy told him? Moving forward, he introduced himself as Steve, telling us he had just graduated and was very new to the facility and his position. *Great,* I thought. *New blood. I bet he will love to take the challenge on.* With him being a younger person, I thought he could relate to Linda better than an older person could. He took lots of notes and measurements and told us to come back in a couple of weeks as they would have a temporary leg for her to put on. *Yes, that's much better,* I thought. Linda felt great when she heard that with physical therapy and the right prosthesis she would be able to walk again.

Back at home we waited. Things were going well, even though I didn't sleep much. In fact, I don't know how I was working three jobs and going to the Clinic as much as I was. I began to notice I was getting heavier and heavier, and I wondered why when I was working like a workhorse. I asked my mother, and her reply was, "Jackie, did you ever see a skinny workhorse?" Okay, that hurt. I guess some people get skinny under stress and others put on weight. Lucky me, huh?

The next year just flew by, and I don't think I picked my head up once to smell the flowers. I was focused on my priorities. Anything extra was a plus. Linda had gotten her prosthesis, but it was a challenge. It took months of physical therapy for her to master her gait. But after all the frustration, she did it. By the time she was walking, my dad had fixed up an older car for her to drive. She got her license, and I was happy she had gotten back her independence as well. She also tried to go back to school her senior year, but we had a few setbacks. Linda was very susceptible to infections, and any little thing could kick one up. They were not just minor infections, either. Once they got into her bloodstream, they went wild. She did earn all her credits to graduate through in-home teaching, but the day of commencement she fell ill, so she couldn't attend. I put on a very nice graduation party for her anyway, and we all celebrated her success in graduating. It was at her graduation party, in fact, that she met Robert, her future husband, through my Aunt Margie—he was her neighbor—and Robert really liked Linda.

Well, next comes another twist.

CHAPTER 5

One day, I was running late to show a home to some prospective buyers. Most times the seller is not home during a showing, but in that particular case, he was and had let the buyers in before me. I hurried in, apologizing for being a few minutes late. Everyone was okay, though; the seller had already shown them around.

After I said goodbye to the buyers, I went in to thank the owner, Rick, for letting us see the house. I was very much in a business mode, so I guess I didn't notice he was flirting with me. I hadn't even thought about dating in years. In fact, I had not been with anyone in four years. However, this man had something else on his mind other than business. He called Peggy, the listing agent—who was also his friend from church and who just so happened to be one of my best friends at my real estate company—and started asking questions about me. He was recently widowed and ready to start dating, and he liked me.

When Peggy called to tell me the news, I was more than surprised. I told her right from the start that I didn't want to date, that I only vaguely remembered him. But day after day, she kept after me to at least meet him. There could be no harm in that, she said, right? I figured it couldn't hurt to have a friend, just a male friend, so I told her she could give him my number. He called me the next evening, again surprising me, I must say, by calling so quickly. We had a very nice talk on the phone and then he asked if I would like to meet him for a drink that coming Saturday at his private German club. I agreed to meet, then I planned my get-out-of-this-date scenario by bribing Linda to wait one hour then call my cell phone and act like there was an emergency and I had to leave fast. I figured one hour should be enough, and I didn't want to appear rude.

Well, that night, getting ready was a little scary. Since my divorce, I hadn't dated anyone after Don from Colorado. *This should be interesting,* I thought as I looked in the mirror and all I saw was a tired-out woman with bags under her eyes. I couldn't understand what this guy even saw in me. But I put on my makeup and jeans, blouse, and blazer, and off I went. He was waiting outside the club when I arrived, which I thought was very nice. And he greeted me with a very light hug then escorted me inside, where we sat at the bar. I wasn't initially aware of it, but it was a club he frequented, and soon I think every person there knew he was on a date. They were aware his wife had died recently and I was his date for the night. I kept noticing a few guys giving him the thumbs up, and that felt creepy. I felt on display to see if I met with approval to date him. It felt odd, but hey, I had fifty minutes to go before the call would come from Linda so I could gracefully end the date. There was only one problem with that plan: I had forgotten to turn the ringer volume up on my phone, so there it was, in my purse, on vibrate.

Anyway, as we began to talk, I became aware that he was a very nice man. We talked about our kids, and he told me about his landscaping business. The more we talked, time just flew. He was so interesting. When my hour was up and Linda began calling my phone according to plan, I of course didn't even hear it down in my purse, vibrating, in the noisy bar. It wasn't until maybe three or four hours later that we ended our date. And when I looked at my phone, Linda had called maybe ten times. When I finally got home, she was worried something may have happened to me. I just laughed and said he was a very nice man and we were having a great conversation and I forgot about time for those few hours.

The next day, Peggy was grilling me at work on how the date had gone. I was brief, saying I didn't even know except that he was polite and we'd had a good conversation.

"Well, when are you seeing him again?" she asked. I just shrugged and said nothing.

"I don't know," I answered. "We never addressed a second date."

A few days went by, and I didn't think much of it. I was so busy in my own life that I didn't know how I would fit a relationship into it, anyway. I hardly had time to sleep, as it was. But a few days later, the phone rang. It was Rick calling to say how much fun he'd had and how much he'd enjoyed talking with me. I felt the same way. He asked if we could do it again, offering to take me out to dinner the following week. I was free, so I accepted. It was early April, and everything was just starting to bloom, the weather was changing, and the air felt so nice.

On the same night I would be going to dinner with Rick, Linda had plans, also, with Robert. Those two seemed to be becoming quite a pair. *I have my eye on that boy. He'd better not try anything,* I thought. Linda seemed happy with him, and it was the first time I had seen Linda so happy.

The week had flown by, and before I knew it, Saturday—the night of my dinner with Rick—had arrived. I knew Rick and I were going to a quaint little restaurant by a lake somewhere on the outskirts of our area. He said being there felt like you were inside a Norman Rockwell painting, so I was excited to see it for that reason as well. It would just be nice to get out and see something new. I didn't get out much, of course. I wore a sundress and brought a light sweater just in case it was chilly. He picked me up that afternoon about four o'clock at my apartment. Rick said it would take about an hour to get to the restaurant, and we wanted to have time to walk around the lake before dinner, as well.

It turned out to be the cutest place I had ever been. And Rick had been right: it did certainly have a Norman Rockwell quality. Flowers were blooming everywhere. Ducks swam in the lake and people of all ages were sitting or walking around it. The restaurant was at least one hundred years old, tidy, and very cozy. We walked and talked for a long while then sat down and had a glass of wine at a table outdoors. Rick had made reservations for seven p.m. because the restaurant was always busy, even during the week. I started to think back on my restaurant and how it had felt to run it. Sure, it was a lot of work, but I'd had a passion for making it successful. I also had a passion to be successful in my new career, having my own business as a real estate agent.

Dinner was just lovely. The atmosphere and food were unbelievable. It was just a perfect evening, and I was glad I went. Once again, Rick dropped me off at my apartment and was a perfect gentleman. I was really beginning to enjoy his company. Although he was nine years my senior, he didn't act old. He had a good soul, and we began spending more and more time together. It started out just as friends. I had never dreamed of another person coming into my life for a serious relationship after my marriage to Joe ended. And on top of that, I had Linda and Joey to think about first. I still wanted my son to come back and live with me. I never lost hope about that for one minute.

Soon thereafter, I celebrated my fortieth birthday at my apartment with a wonderful surprise party from Linda, complete with cake, treats, and even decorations. Some of the family came, including my son, Joey, and Linda had also invited my new special friend, Rick. That was a happy time for me, and turning forty felt great. I had never been afraid of getting older. I was just happy to be healthy and alive.

Along with my job's success increasing as I brought in more sales, Linda continued to get healthier. Since meeting Robert, she was happier than I'd seen her in years. Months later, Linda told me she wanted to move out. *What? Why?* I thought. She said she and my stepsister Christine wanted to rent an apartment that was close to my apartment. Linda was bringing in money from her social security, and I didn't need it; I was generating enough money to live on. I was apprehensive about her making the move because I always felt that no one could take care of her like I could. Boy, was I thinking wrong. I remember back when I was her age at nineteen. I knew I couldn't hold her back. I had to let her fly, let her have a life. So I agreed to help her find an apartment as well as help her buy things to furnish it, and she and my sister put together a cute place. Then it was my turn to back off. She knew I would always be there for her if she needed anything.

One day, right after Linda moved out and I was feeling alone again, I got a call from my son. He was now a freshman in high school, having problems living with his father, and asked if he could come back to live with me.

Tears filled my eyes as I said, "YES! When do you want to come?"

When Joey replied, "ASAP?" I was so happy and surprised. I had waited years to hear those words.

He moved in that Saturday. I had just enough time to clean the bedroom Linda had occupied. While he got settled in, I worried about how he would feel around me since he'd had free rein at his dad's house for all those years. However, I shouldn't have worried; he was amazing, and we sort of just picked up where we had left off. I asked no questions and he offered no information. We simply went from that day forward. He had always been a great child. Since birth, he had never given me a hard time or even one problem. He was perfect—honestly. I could never have asked for a more perfect son. In every way, he was the most respectable young man I had ever met. I was so proud of him. When he moved in, I was the happiest mother in the world. I had my son back. I wasn't going to let anything stand in the way of us from that time on. My focus had been on Linda for so many years because of her illness, and Joey's needs were often put aside unintentionally.

With Linda, the more I gave to her, the more she took, the less she respected me, and the more she treated me terribly. I was her punching ball, so to speak. She blamed me often for her tumor disease and for the doctors not finding the third tumor sooner, and I blamed myself for a long time as well. But as I stated earlier, the main problem was the rarity of her disease. Unfortunately, back in the 1980s when her first tumor surfaced, the doctors assumed it was a fatty tumor. Since there was not enough research on desmoid tumors at the time, they couldn't do much with it but remove it and hope it didn't reoccur. But after three reoccurrences, it now became very evident that something big was happening. We just hadn't found it early enough. And for over thirty years, I lived with that guilt, with all of the *what ifs*. Only with years of counseling did I learn to comprehend the magnitude of her sickness, to realize that it was not my fault the medical community had not recognized it soon enough or treated it effectively at first. If it weren't for counseling at that time, I may have broken down mentally; there were times I just didn't want to live. But I prayed, I prayed hard, and I managed to stay strong with the grace of our Lord Jesus Christ. I put the whole matter in the Lord's hands and decided it was much greater than me. I handed it over to Him.

During the remainder of 1996, after Linda had moved out and Joey had moved in, we had a lot going on.

Joey did his typical things kids do in high school. He was very active during school and attended activities such as dances. He also had a part-time job, and I never had a problem with him adhering to his curfew. I was so glad to have him back home, the very thing I'd waited so long to have.

Also during that year, Rick and I continued to date, and by Christmastime he popped the question about getting married. He had sold his home and wanted to initially move in with me, and then we would buy a home together after we married. I was so taken in by all his attention at the time, but in hindsight I realize I should have gotten to know him better before I took the leap again.

We married in January 1997 in a small cottage in Mill Creek Park, with just close friends and family in attendance. Our children stood up for us, and my son gave me away. It was all very nice. Looking back, however, I remember we started fighting right after we married. Rick was a very staunch German man, sweet at times but set in his ways. We were still living in my apartment during January, an off season for his landscaping business.

Before we married, I didn't know he took winters off—remember, we'd only met in April and married in January. I was taken aback. While I was working during the winter in the cold and snow, selling and listing homes, he sat at home on the computer. He claimed he had paperwork and things to catch up on for the following season. To me, it just meant he would not be bringing in any money during that time. He never offered to help with rent, utilities, or any of the other monthly expenses after he moved in and we were married. He would periodically buy some groceries, but that was all. Everything else to run that household and to take care of my personal expenses was on me, alone. His reasoning was that since I had handled the expenses alone before he came into the picture, I could continue to do so. At that point, I should have recognized the red flags.

After a couple months of that living arrangement, I started feeling resentment. I could no longer contain my emotions. The signs were probably always there; the problem was I was blinded. I let a little attention from a man pull at my heartstrings. I didn't go into the marriage with my eyes wide open. Instead, I went in heart first, and that was a wrong move. We had never discussed finances or the specifics of how we planned to merge our lives.

One thing that should have been a cause for doubt was when he wanted me to sign a prenuptial agreement one week before our marriage. He wanted to make sure that if the marriage didn't work out, the twenty-thousand-dollar profit from the sale of his house would go back to him and I would not be able to touch his business, either. In addition, according to the agreement, I had to have a one-hundred-thousand-dollar life-insurance policy in place with him as the beneficiary. He, too, had the same policy with me as his beneficiary, but I know that any level-headed woman would have run at the first demand alone. At the time, I thought our marriage was going to be for life, so why would I worry about such a thing?

What was I thinking?

It seemed like right out of the gate we had issues. We weren't merging as husband and wife; I was taking care of him. He didn't even have a vehicle to use, only his fertilizing van that he'd put in storage for the winter. Also, after we got married, Rick had sold the car his wife had driven—he thought we could just share mine.

What? As a realtor, I had to have my own car, a necessity for my business. I wasn't going to share that.

As the winter went by, we started looking for a new home. It took months to find one we both liked, so in May we finally found a house and bought it. It was not a new home and much smaller than the home I had shared with Joe in Colorado, but it was cute. It needed a lot of updating, and we thought we could do that over the years. I had started yet another new venture, with a new husband. I thought that no marriage was perfect, but I was going to give this one a new shot and give it all I had to give.

When we bought the house, Rick had already started back to work with his lawn-maintenance company. When I met him, he'd had a crew that worked for him and he seemed like a very motivated businessman running a lawn-care company. I didn't realize that after we got married he would cut back and become a one-man show. He had his son work with him whenever the son showed up, but otherwise he did all the grass cutting and fertilization himself. I really didn't know much about his finances because we'd never discussed how much he made—my second mistake.

Then came tax time. I was bringing in between fifty-five and sixty thousand dollars a year, and I was surprised to see he showed only eighteen thousand dollars in profit for himself. I was more than mortified to find out I was the one who was going to carry the house and most of our expenses. That was going to be a problem. For starters, I didn't think I had signed up for that. But I hadn't thought to ask the question. They say money can't buy you love, but let's get real: financial security is important at a certain time in a woman's life. I had been single for five years and was just fine on my own. I didn't feel I should be taking care of a man, and I sure didn't want to be the primary bread winner.

As it turned out, Rick was willing to pay for some food as well as the house payment, which was seven hundred dollars per month, taxes included. I was to take care of everything else, including my hospitalization, any bills pertaining to the house, and any credit cards, remaining food, and my personal expenses. *Wow,* I thought, *this is not what I expected.* I was very resentful, and I think our marriage was doomed from the start. I can't say I ever felt a real bond in that marriage. Once I was in it, I just tried to make the best I could of it.

Around the time we moved into our house, Linda dropped the news that she and Robert were planning to get married in November of that year, 1998. I had mixed feelings about it, but she seemed so happy, and who was I to take away whatever happiness she was to have in life? They claimed they loved each other, and by that time they had already rented an apartment together and were living there.

Because Linda had gone through so much in her short life, I finally accepted that if marrying Robert was what she wanted, I was not going to stop her happiness, and we started to plan the wedding. I was so busy that year with everything—work, redoing our new house, and planning the wedding—that I didn't have time to focus on much more than that. My son, Joe, had moved with us into our new home, and he of course was still busy with his own life. Yes, we were all quite busy that year.

Linda's wedding was lovely, and I was so proud the day I saw her walking down the aisle with her father. She had mastered the use of her prosthesis. She looked like a lovely princess, beaming from ear to ear. She had proven wrong the prosthetist at the Cleveland Clinic who said she would never be able to walk again.

Can't is not a word I use or had ever let Linda use.

With tears in my eyes and gratitude to God, Linda did it—she had overcome her obstacles. What a blessing the Lord had given her. There was never one time during her whole sickness that I blamed God. I needed Him more at that point than ever. Without Him in my life, I don't think I could have had the strength I needed. I never thought I would see the day Linda would be able to walk down the aisle, but with God's grace she was now marrying her new husband, her best friend in the world.

With every bump, trial, or obstacle there is a reason, and we must learn and grow from it. To this day, I still don't understand why certain people suffer such hardships while others seem to skip through life with no major disruptions. They say God doesn't give us more than we can handle. I happen to think the Lord chooses the people he does to handle these heavy trials not because we can handle it, but because we have something to gain from it if we get the message. He's not punishing us; he's trying to have us open our faith to give our troubles to Him and trust that He will handle things the way He sees fit. Now that may seem difficult for us as humans to comprehend, but nothing happens by coincidence. I think the book of our life was already written, and until we get into that place within ourselves to understand that we are not in charge and to trust the Lord Jesus Christ, we will wander through life in a fog.

Soon after Rick and I bought the house, I gave Robert and Linda my old computer and I purchased a new one. I figured they would like it and could use it. I never realized that by giving it to them, I would start them on the road to going into the computer business. I guess after I gave Robert the computer, he didn't sleep for days—he was so intent upon learning all he could about it. It piqued his interest in building, repairing, and selling computers.

He and Linda then started buying and selling computer parts at flea markets with their first income-tax refund. For nearly two years, they made a living that way. Then one day, my stepdad loaned them enough money to open their first business, a computer business.

In those days, Linda and Robert were very focused on building the business. They worked day and night getting it started. I thought how blessed she was to be able to rise above all her trials and find love, get married, and become a businesswoman. She was a strong woman and determined to make their business work. And they did very well. They built a successful business in our town, and I was very proud of them.

Well, with Joe eventually off to college and Linda married, I focused on updating the house. Rick and I were working through our first couple years of marriage. He still was not over his late wife, and I think he married me too soon after her passing. It was only a year after her death that we got married—another red flag. He claimed he had grieved while she was dying and that he had been ready to move on, but his actions showed otherwise. As I think back, Rick was more infatuated with me and my job than he was in love with me. I was a successful realtor, and he liked the status it gave him. He liked when I would meet him at his German club after work for a drink; he liked seeing me dressed up and businesslike, showing me off to his friends at the bar. I never liked going to his club/bar. I didn't like sitting at a bar for hours. I liked to have a couple glasses of white wine, and then I would get antsy and want to leave. He could sit there for hours, drinking his Beck's beer and talking to the guys, so I would just leave and go home.

Was he in love with me? No, not really. But he didn't want to live alone and he knew he could have a better life if he married me. But as I look back, I realize I wasn't in love with him either. I guess we were just two lonely people who decided to get married because they didn't want to be alone. Yet another big red flag.

I always made dinner for Rick when I wasn't out showing homes. But he, on the other hand, would usually make something for himself when I was working late nights but never have anything ready for me. That hurt. He wasn't complaining about me working late, but how hard could it have been to make something for the two of us?

The more the years went by and the more we had repairs done on the house, I realized I was paying for everything. Oh sure, he chipped in and paid for a few of the repairs, but for the most part they were my responsibility. I became more and more resentful. Why did I have to be the one who had to work all year long, make the money, and handle all the major things that took place? Big red flag. We really didn't share a marriage. It was like being friends with benefits. Anything that had to do with me was my responsibility. When Linda got married, for example, he didn't offer anything towards the wedding. Our monies were separate, our bank accounts were separate, even insurances were separate. It was my responsibility to make enough to cover whatever expenses came up. When Joe graduated from high school and I put on a graduation party for him, it was my responsibility once again. Rick, again, never offered anything. His theory was that they were my kids and why should he have to contribute anything to their graduations, weddings, baby showers, and so on? It was my responsibility, he told me. You would think the least he could have done would be to pick up the slack with the overhead on the house. But no, he didn't budge. He paid his seven hundred dollars per month, took care of his business, and I did the rest to keep the household running.

Now I must admit, after five years of conversations about how I felt this was not how a marriage should be, he would just leave and go to the bar when the subject came up. He said he hated my nagging. But I never thought I would be in a marriage where everything I did or needed was my total responsibility. I worked very hard and did well financially, and I always felt that when you are married you have a partnership together. But Rick was not contributing equally in our marriage. He was not treating me like a wife and a real life partner. He said he hated my nagging.

I knew that marriage was over years before it ended. We did try counseling for a short time with the minister of his church. That didn't go well. Rick felt he didn't have to change in any way, so he continued to live his life and I lived mine. We simply cohabitated. You see, when his last wife died, he was stuck in a financial bind. He vowed never to be put in that situation again, so before he married me, he consulted with an attorney to make sure he protected himself financially. The problem was we were doomed before we started.

At the same time I was going through all the drama with Rick, Linda had given birth to two sons back to back—literally. My two first grandsons were only thirteen months apart. My daughter carried two very healthy sons to term. A miracle and a blessing, as I see it.

Her first pregnancy was easy for her. She was walking well with her prosthetic leg, she'd actually lost fifty pounds during the pregnancy, and she wasn't sick at all. Her health seemed like it was improving daily.

I had the most beautiful baby shower for her. It was such an exciting time, getting ready for the baby, that the nine months went by so fast. Before we knew it, Linda was getting ready for the birth. Her husband swore he couldn't and wouldn't be present at the birth because he hated the sight of blood. Linda asked me to be there with her. *Okay,* I thought. But I had never seen a C-section birth, so I didn't know what to expect. I sat behind a curtain, holding Linda's hand, waiting patiently until the doctors told me I could stand up and look over the curtain.

As I sat there, I remembered back to the years before, watching over Linda's sickbed as she was administered her last rites. The thought of losing your child to a horrific disease and not being able to help was more than I thought I could handle. But by the grace of the Lord, He gave me strength. The strength I needed to walk through that dark time and now at this moment to get the chance to see my grandson coming into the world. *Wow!* The feeling was too much to put into words.

I feel the hardest time to have faith is when we are faced with the worst of times. We are humans, and when faced with diversities that we can't control and ones that we are not comfortable with, we tend to blame someone, anyone. And God is often the first one people tend to blame. The

"Why me?" syndrome. I say today, "Why not?" It's not the Lord who is punishing us. I don't believe He makes bad things happen to good people.

We must accept that sometimes things just happen. And it's not the act of the situation; it's the reaction to it that helps us accept and trust in God's will. It's so spiritual, and I have had an opportunity to have experienced it firsthand.

When the doctors finally said it was time for me to look over the curtain in the delivery room, I saw the most beautiful miracle of my life. A brand-new life, a grandson, and to me he was perfect. The doctors pulled him, a healthy ten-pound baby boy, from her belly. I was watching and experiencing God's greatest miracle, the miracle of life.

Although I couldn't have foreseen it that day of her first son's birth, by the time of this writing Linda would have gone through over fifty surgeries, a two-week coma, and being given her last rites. God was not ready for her yet; she had a purpose. What her purpose was to be, I don't know, but we all have one. It's up to each person to figure it out and pass it on. All I knew at that moment was a feeling of amazement, gratitude, and humility while tears of joy ran down my face. I had cried for so many years for Linda during all the trials she'd had to face, and now we were looking at a brand-new life that the Lord gave her to raise. I saw it as one of the most spiritual times I would ever experience. And to top it off, he was born on his mother's twenty-first birthday, November twenty-fourth, in 2000.

When the nurses brought this new little life, Anthony Joseph Santos, to me to hold for the first time, I was so nervous that my adrenaline was out of control. I asked the doctor to hold onto the baby because I thought I might drop him. I was crying and shaking at the same time. It's true what they say about a grandmother's love, that you can't compare it to anything else—he was the most beautiful baby I'd ever seen. *My first-born grandson.* Those words resonated in my mind. I never imagined that moment could ever happen to Linda, that she would beat all the odds the doctors had predicted, but the doctors can't control God's amazing miracles.

I was now trying to juggle being in a marriage, selling real estate, running back and forth to my daughter's house to help with her babies, and taking care of her when she was repeatedly hospitalized. I never stopped running. I guess that's how my marriage lasted with Rick for the five years it did. I was always involved and tried to stay busy.

At the time when so many things were going on and I felt like I couldn't possibly juggle anything else, my stepfather developed a patent on a method concept. It was not a tangible item but rather a concept to reduce bulk mailing costs by selling advertising space on the inside cover of the pieces. The concept would be applied to large mailings. It was a complicated process and one that took up a lot of my time for nearly five years. My mother, a friend named Denise, and I were the ones about to embark upon that journey. It was a great idea, and I am a believer that if you believe hard enough, anything is possible. Thus, with everything I already had on my plate, I just added a new project.

I was still managing that venture along with all the other things I was working on. We worked on a shoestring with little or no money, walked a lot of miles knocking on doors and promoting the concept, had more meetings with different major companies than I can remember, and attended many seminars throughout the country. It seemed the more we tried, the more obstacles would get in our way. For example, Linda was in and out of the hospital so many times after her second child was born. Each time she was sick, I would drop the ball with the business venture and run to take care of her and the children. It seemed I was always either in a hospital or watching the kids. Linda's husband did nothing but go to work and that was about it. I never lost sight of my goals, however. I just tried to prioritize everything and decided I would have to be there for Linda and the kids. It was my responsibility, I kept convincing myself.

That went on year after year. No sooner would Linda get back home and things get back to a new normal than she would be sick again. My life was not my own. I just didn't realize it at the time I was going through it. But I never gave up. I always figured a way that I could do anything. Looking back, I realize that was not such a great attitude as I lost focus of what should have been important to me. If I wasn't traveling to promote the concept patent, I was working on real estate or taking care of my grandchildren and Linda. I felt at times I was on a hamster wheel, running and running but not knowing where I was going, with my heart always racing.

I didn't know it then, but I was living in survival mode. I needed to be strong, I needed to take charge, and I had to always be the one who had all the answers and who could handle anything thrown in my way. I was a control freak. I never thought of saying "No!" or even delegating tasks or responsibilities to another person. I felt I could handle it all on my own.

What a joke that was.

By 2000, Joey was getting ready to graduate from high school. He wanted to go to college, but in all his years of high school, Joey never really focused on the scholastic side of it. He got by and passed, but I never thought he had a real passion for furthering his education, so when he came to me and asked if I could help him get into a college, I was totally surprised. Of course I would help him. I questioned whether he really wanted to go to college to learn or just to party, but I had to give him the benefit of the doubt. He was maturing, and if he wanted to go, he should at least have a shot at it, I felt.

So off he went in the fall of 2000 to Toledo University. Setting him up in his dorm was a bittersweet moment. He was the last to leave the nest. And yes, I did feel a sense of loneliness. I had waited so long to have him come back to me, and now those four short years had flown by. I did realize that our children are just loaned to us and our job is to raise them to fly confidently out of the nest and into the real world. *He'll be back,* I thought. *It's not for good. I love him enough to give him the space to grow.*

Well, as it turned out, he was back every Friday. He drove three hours every Friday to spend the weekend at home, where I washed his clothes, cooked for him, and always made cookies for him to take back to school. He told me the guys in his dorm always looked forward to him bringing back the cookies.

During the winter break at Christmastime of his freshman year at Toledo, Joey found out his cousin Allen, who was also his roommate at college, got sick. They didn't know exactly what was wrong with him until tests showed he had leukemia. My son was devastated, so much so that he didn't want to go back to school after the winter break. I didn't want to force him to go back, because I knew that if his mind was not in the right place his studies would suffer. He stayed out for a few months until one day, he told me he was ready to go back and finish the year. I was proud of his strength and determination, and I knew it was important that he had made his own choice to return to school when he was ready.

Allen was not only Joe's first cousin but his best friend. They were the same age and had grown up together since they were babies. Eventually a bone-marrow donor was found, and Allen received a transplant. I am happy to say he is doing great today and is cancer free.

After Joe finished the school year, he decided he wanted to stay closer to home, so he transferred to a local university. He didn't want to move back home, so I helped him get an apartment close to the campus. When he took all his furniture out of his bedroom, then, I had an empty room. I decided I could either make it a spare room or a baby's room so my grandson could stay with me. *Nursery—YES!* I decided, and I went on a mission to visit any garage sale and used-furniture shop to get everything I needed to have a bedroom for Anthony. When I was finished furnishing and decorating the room, it was darling. I even had clothes there for him, so whenever Linda wanted me to watch the baby, I was prepared. I loved it! I don't think I ever said no to her needs when it came to babysitting.

Linda was now getting more ill. The second pregnancy really took a toll on her health. She was sick the entire nine months with the second child. Her diabetes took a turn for the worse, and she was no longer able to wear her prosthetic leg. After the baby was born, she had even more serious problems. With all the hormones going through her body, it had made her stump grow a few inches. That was bad because the doctors had to go in and re-amputate a few inches of the leg. From that surgery, many infections set in, and Linda had to be hospitalized several times. PICC (peripherally inserted central catheter) lines were something I became used to, as I had to administer her antibiotics intravenously.

As I kept both grandsons a lot during Linda's hospital stays, I was glad I had my own nursery set up at my house with everything the babies needed. Since Linda's sons were so close in age, they were almost like twins. I had a crib for one and a day bed for the other. Also, I had a baby gate on the door. They even had their own playroom. I loved every moment of it.

Thank God I was self-employed, too. I don't know how I managed all of it. I was great at juggling balls, as they say. Along with taking care of the babies, I was back and forth to the hospital, during which times Linda had many surgeries, and when needed, I stayed at the hospital with her. In addition, of course, I had to continue to work at selling homes, to help develop my stepfather's patent, to fix up the house we bought, and to stay married.

CHAPTER 6

Looking back on my life after all these years, I see that the one thing that always took priority over everything else was Linda. I put her first above everyone and everything, even my own needs. I was on a mission to keep her alive no matter what it took. When I total it up, I spent literally more than twenty-five years in a hospital. If she checked in for a week, month, or many months, I checked in and never left till she left. I always felt that if I was there, I would protect her and nothing would happen to her. My life was dedicated to her illness. I don't remember how I did it. I just knew I had to be strong. No surgery that Linda had was ever easy. There were always complications, and infections always set in. We never knew how the outcome would be.

I remember one May when Linda's good leg, her only complete leg, went bad and they had to operate on it. It took till September to heal. I stayed with her and took care of her and her children, who were then five and four years old. I know for a fact that God does give us the strength to cope in times of need. I am proof of that. I could have never done all of that by myself. He carried me and gave me His strength to do the job. I give all the praise and glory to Him. I am just a human, and I could never have had withstood that storm alone.

Well, the sickness went from a knee surgery to lymphedema—a swelling that happens when the lymphatic system is not working properly—that whole summer. Understand that she was bed bound, with one leg amputated and the good leg not able to be used during the nearly three months it took to heal. So it was a very big challenge to care for her. But with the help of nurses and aides and myself, we set up a hospital room in her family room and the kids were able to spend time with their mother as she healed. I always made sure they were all well taken care of and tried to do things with the boys that their mother couldn't do.

As months went by, lymphedema developed in both the good leg and the amputee leg. I went with her to treatments to reduce the swelling and hopefully get it cured. It was then about six months after the last surgery.

While the good leg became functional again, the leg that was amputated was unfortunately overtaken by the lymphedema. After consulting with her surgeons at the

Cleveland Clinic, the team of physicians decided there was no option but to amputate the leg to the hip. That was the third amputation to that leg. But if they hadn't removed the lymphedema, it would have been very dangerous for her. By that time, the leg was swollen to at least five times its normal size. It was an awful time. I was sick to my stomach yet somehow stronger in ways I never knew I could be. Yes, I was concerned, but I was handling it much differently that time. I guess the more the years went by, the better I was at handling these setbacks and illnesses. I was getting older and probably more mature and just went with the flow. I almost wasn't surprised by any of it any more, as sad as that sounds.

I loved the Lord but didn't understand. I was tired of crying, I was tired of praying, I was tired of yelling at Him for Linda's suffering, I was just flat-out exhausted. Why couldn't He go pick on someone else for a change?

Jackie Dobrosky

I read the Book of Job in the Bible so many times and felt like God was testing me like he tested Job. But mine was going on for a lifetime.

I was becoming more and more bitter toward God then. "Look, I am not Job!" I would scream out loud. I wanted so badly to stop praying, to stop talking to Him. I thought, *What good is it doing?* I questioned my faith more than a few times. But after each tantrum, I would always need to talk to Him. In my heart, I knew I couldn't get through it without Him. I just didn't understand His plan. I couldn't see the whole picture of what was to be someday.

We had been through more than fifty surgeries, some more major than others but together there were many. Now the additional amputation would mean she would never be able to walk again, never effectively use a prosthesis. She was just in her twenties and had two little children. She was beyond depressed. I tried to help uplift her spirits, but how could I when I couldn't even understand why everything was happening to her? I was angry, I was bitter, and I could not understand God's will. I questioned Him again and again. I became so depressed, as well.

By then, Linda had lived with such pain, pain I could not and will never understand. All the doctors could do was keep her comfortable, and that meant they gave her whatever pain medications it took to give her some relief. And since she was only fifteen at the time of her first surgery and now approaching her thirties, she had become addicted to those pain medications. I could not do anything about it, and she couldn't get out of pain, so they kept the medications coming. I do have bittersweet feelings about them. At the time, the medications meant relief for Linda, but as the years progressed she built up a tolerance to them and needed more and more to keep the pain levels down.

Jackie Dobrosky

When she was admitted to have the hip disarticulation, it felt like we were going through the amputation for the first time. The feelings were the same. She was so depressed, and her husband was disengaged with the whole thing. Robert was never one to show a lot of emotion. In the ten years my daughter was married, I don't ever think I understood his ice-cold nature. But once again, I stayed at the hospital with Linda and sent Robert home to take care of his kids. It's hard to remember how long we stayed in the hospital that time—maybe a couple of weeks.

When Linda did come home, we had the routine perfected. Everything was set up again in the family room: hospital bed, medical equipment, nurses already scheduled, and my bags packed to stay at her house. Next, an infection set into the area of the hip disarticulation, and it had to be opened completely in order to heal from the inside out. The medical team used a wound vac on it, and I was taught how to change it. Between myself and the nurses, it took a few months for it to heal. During the healing period, a vein hemorrhaged one day while the wound was being changed and we had to call 911 to have Linda taken back to the hospital. It was a short stay, and she returned home to continue to heal.

After that surgery, the healing process and complications were taking a toll on her strength, both mentally and physically. She began taking pain medications to kill not only the physical pain but the emotional pain as well.

I know she loved her children and also her husband, but she was getting too dependent on the pills and I feel they were affecting how she was acting and relating to life. Everything seemed to revolve around her and for good reasons—she was the sick one. And sometimes when you have been out of control of your own life, the only thing you have control over is to deaden your true emotions. Therefore, while her use of the pain pills started off innocently, it eventually escalated out of control.

Many years before Linda became addicted to it, I was concerned the medication was becoming a problem, but how could she live without the pills when they kept chipping away at her body parts? I don't think a year went by that she was not in a surgery of some sort. It was a living nightmare and thus not completely her fault she became dependent upon the medications and sometimes took more than what was prescribed. I was helpless. I would have done anything at that time to take her pain away, but I couldn't; it wasn't my pain.

That's when I started to question God. "God, if you are a God of mercy, where are you? Why are you allowing this to happen?"

I became bitter. I thought not only Linda was being punished, but the kids were as well. They knew nothing about their mother other than she had always been sick since the day they were born. Why did they have to suffer, too, watching their mother in pain and lying in a hospital bed all the time?

As strong as I had been all through those years, I was starting to break down, seeking out counseling for strength and to find a way to accept my new normal life.

It was a never-ending journey with Linda. Even after she was a grown woman, I couldn't leave her. She knew I was there, day or night, whenever she needed me. And boy, did she need me. With Linda wheelchair bound, I would come daily to help wash clothes, clean the house, make bottles, and bathe the babies. It was nearly impossible for her to manage those tasks alone. I know you are probably wondering where her husband was during all of this. Oh, he was there, but in body only. I started to resent his aloof attitude; he did nothing to help. Yes, he worked, but after that he was done for the day. And that was the most he did while his sons were infants.

Jackie Dobrosky

He and Linda were both only twenty-one when they got married, and Robert didn't come from the best of families—pretty much uneducated and mostly without ambition. He married Linda knowing she had only one leg, and I do believe he loved her. I just don't believe he knew what he was getting into, and it was much more than he was capable of handling. Her sickness ruled their life. Also, they had kids right away, so they never had the chance to really enjoy a normal married life as a young couple. In addition to that, he had to deal with a constantly sick wife, running his business alone, and Linda's problem with pills. I think he couldn't handle it and just gave up. Now, I am not giving him props for that as I think he is, in my books, a "deadbeat dad." He left my daughter and the kids. He just walked out the door—just as simple as that—and never turned around, and it's been eight years.

At that point, I had been through too much in my life and had had enough on my plate. My marriage was becoming more and more challenging and difficult. If I'd wanted merely a roommate, I would have put an ad in the paper to find one. It was the year 2002 and I was done. Rick was in his fifties, and I was certain he was not going to change. He had sold his business to his biggest competitor and then he turned around and went to work for the same man for a measly ten dollars an hour. That was the straw that broke the camel's back, for me, and if I had stayed with him, I would have been miserable for the rest of my life because I already resented him. I didn't care if it was my second marriage. There was no saving it.

It had taken me five years to figure out that man was using me, and I would not take it anymore. It had really been a business deal from the beginning, and we handled it as a business deal when we divorced. This time, I did not leave during the split and we had a very amicable divorce process. We went through the house and evenly dispersed our possessions. We put the house on the market and sold it in one day, reaping a hefty profit.

From start to finish, it took only forty-five days to finalize our divorce. That final day in court, I thought to myself, *This is it. I am going to finish the rest of my journey alone. I will never make the same mistake again. I am just not the marrying type, and I will not accept being used.* I had been looking for love but not in the right way. I needed then to open my eyes and see things for what they were instead of through rose-colored lenses. I wanted to be loved so badly that I was choosing husbands for the wrong reason. All the red flags were there, but at forty-five years old, I was so tired of being alone in our marriage. Why couldn't I get it right?

The day we closed the sale of the house, we both went to the bank to cash the check. Rick gave it to the teller and said, "Take that twenty thousand dollars out of the check first and put it on my side." This was per the prenuptial agreement, and the remaining balance was split between us fifty-fifty. I walked away from that with twelve thousand six hundred dollars. I remember that figure so well because by that time I had already put an offer on a condo I'd found and was waiting on the proceeds from the closing to finalize the purchase on it. The day I closed on my new condo and got the key was the best day of my life.

I started to once again to rebuild my life. Hey, I was getting good at this! I moved on like nothing even happened. In fact, not a tear was shed by me. Just like the marriage itself, the divorce was more like a business transaction. I fulfilled my obligation regarding the prenuptial agreement and still walked away from that marriage with a lot more than from my first marriage, so this time I was in a lot better financial shape. I was excited to put my condo in my name only. I determined I would never lose anything again because of a man. *I am finished with men and marriages.*

Jackie Dobrosky

I was living in my condo after my divorce, working in real estate, and after my son, Joe, finished college he moved back in with me. He was a pleasure to live with. He worked and I worked, and we would have dinner together in the evenings. There were nights when Joe and I would sit down to eat, and I would just look at him. He was about twenty-two at the time. I loved him so much. With tears in my eyes, the only regret I ever hold in my life is not being able to be there for him at certain important times of his life while he was growing up. I lived in and out of hospitals with Linda's sickness for over twenty-five years. It's not that Joe was neglected at all. In fact, he was well taken care of by his father and family. It was my absence that breaks my heart. As his mother, I didn't nurture him in the way a mother would nurture her child, but my circumstance was so different.

My ex-husband was not exactly great at co-parenting, especially when it interfered with his life. Don't rock his boat or his lifestyle. He was just a visitor. I think it took my son growing up to fully appreciate why I did things the way I did. I wish things could have been different. It still breaks my heart to think of all the missed years we had.

I'll never forget one time when my son broke his arm. It was at the same time Linda was in the hospital when she lost her leg. I couldn't be there to take him to the hospital, so his aunt took him and the doctor put his arm in a cast. To this day, I feel guilty for not being there. Joe and I have talked about it and have made peace with the fact that at times he felt neglected but now as a grown man of thirty-eight and a father of a wonderful, beautiful son, he understands why I did what I did. It took him being a parent himself to realize that the love you have for your children is priceless and you would do anything to make sure they are safe and healthy. I am so proud of the man he turned out to be.

After a long sabbatical from work to care for Linda, I was going back. I had taken out a second mortgage on my home to get by, and I had maxed out all my credit cards to live. I needed to go back to work and sell some houses. It was coming into a slow period in the real estate market around Thanksgiving and through the holidays. I was scraping by financially but always managed to pay my bills.

Each year, Christmas Eve was my holiday, I always made our Christmas celebration special, and that year was no different. Even though my condo wasn't large, it worked fine with a Christmas tree and by opening up the dining room table to have our Christmas dinner. By then, my parents had moved to Florida permanently. So really it was just a small group of family, including my sister, her children, my children, and my grandchildren. It was a joyous holiday, and I was so happy and thankful that finally we had some happiness and health.

My Unexpected Journey

The first of the year flew by, with everyone going back to their own lives. Linda went back to work, and the kids were in day care. Things seemed ok, but I didn't see much of Linda as I was trying to get my real estate business back on its feet. When I did see her, I started noticing her strange behavior, and every time I would stop by her business, she was either too occupied to see me or she was gone. After a while, I asked her to meet me for lunch and as we spoke, I noticed she was high. I knew by now there was a real problem, but she became very indifferent when I questioned her odd behavior.

A while later, I became aware that things were not going well at her business, bills were not being paid, and her spending was out of control. I had a talk with her husband at one point, and he was totally fed up with her. Her only job was to pay the bills and take care of payroll at their business. She was not only falling behind on that, but her own personal bills were behind as well, and things were falling apart financially. She was distant and always hanging out with her sister in law, and they were shopping all the time.

Robert, her husband, was not a strong man or even a very smart man. He really fell into the computer business because my family set him up financially. But we accepted the fact Linda said she loved him and she felt no one else would love her with one leg, so she settled. Now, they had a flourishing computer business that repaired and sold computers. They had run it successfully for many years, but no longer was it producing like it did before.

It wasn't until Linda became addicted to the pills that her life started to fall apart. Every time any of the family members brought it to her attention, it just drove a wedge further and further into our relationships. She distanced herself from everyone because she didn't want us to question her about what she did in her life.

Her marriage was falling apart, their business was failing, and it seemed there was nothing I could do to stop the falling knife.

It was around March that my stepdad called me from Florida, asking me if I could come to Florida and take care of my mother, who had recently had hip surgery. My stepdad had to fly out to Texas for work, and he needed someone to be with Mom to take care of her while he was away. At that time, I was having a slow spell at work and I was totally burned out from living every day of my life worrying about Linda's drug problem. I could do nothing to fix it and had tried the best I could, so I took the week off to fly to Florida, help with my mother, and just get away for a bit. I needed the break, and I loved being in Florida—my heart was always there.

After I returned to Ohio, I remember a time when my kids told me I should get a life for myself. I had been single for three years and had really wrapped myself up in Linda, my grandsons, and my job. My kids felt I needed more in my life than what I had. I did, however, find the time to date although not much. I did date a few men—nothing serious—and mostly kept my private life private. I think the kids planted a seed in my head when they said, "Get a life, Mom." I think what they meant was to get a dog or join a women's group or start a knitting group. Who knows? Anyway, I don't know how I decided to take control of my life; maybe it was the conversation with the kids.

I never liked Ohio, and the winters killed me emotionally. I don't like snow or gloomy weather. I knew the real estate market was doing well in Florida and decided to make one of the most important decisions of my life. I was going to move back to Florida—on my own. It was my fourth time moving back to the Sunshine State. The first three times I'd never wanted to leave but had to leave each time not by my choice. So at last, I was going alone. My parents had a condo, and I stayed with them until I became re-licensed in Florida.

CHAPTER 7

After fifteen years of selling real estate at the same company in Ohio, I quit my job, put my condo up for sale, and moved away. I had spent so many years in hospitals, I was completely burned out. Linda was in a place I was not happy with; she was struggling with her addiction to pain pills. I couldn't change her or even help, because she didn't want it. She was in total denial, and I didn't want to watch her destroying herself. I couldn't get her husband's help, and I had nothing left inside to give; I had given all I had. I had been fighting to keep her alive for twenty-five years. I fought my hardest, and I tried with everything I had inside to help her, but she would not accept it and said I was interfering in her life. According to her, she was fine and she knew what she was doing.

I realized that if I wanted to have a life, too—and I wasn't getting any younger—I had to let go. I guess I figured if I didn't take the chance of moving to a place that I loved and wanted to live my whole life, I would regret sacrificing my own happiness as I knew how short life was and how many years I had already sacrificed. So yes, I decided to leave and start my life again. Heck, I was used to starting again. In fact, I think I perfected it.

Linda had a husband, and as she said, she had her own life to live the way she wanted. I had put my time in and had given it my all. I couldn't change her, and I needed her to see the road she was heading down was not a healthy one. But still she just asked me to let her live her own life and thanked me for all I had done. I prayed and prayed and then decided I needed to break it off and let her grow up, hoping she would see her current road was not the way to true happiness and that one day she would not be able to break her addiction.

When I moved to Florida, my son, Joe, was living in my Ohio condo, which was then on the market. It took about six months to sell, and he stayed there until it did. Once in Florida at my parents' condo, I stayed in a spare room, which had a bed and a desk. I did nothing but study and go to real estate school. By the time I finished school and was licensed in Florida, I got word that I had sold the condo.

While I was in real estate school, I met a new friend, one who would turn out to be my new best friend in Florida. We met one day on a break from class, and it was an instant friendship. Sue had just moved from Canada during the same time I had moved from Ohio. As soon as I sold my condo, we decided we would move in together as roommates and rented a place on the beach, because our only stipulation for our rental was it must be on the ocean. Call it a mid-life crisis or not, but I was getting ready to turn fifty and I'd wanted to live on the beach my whole life. Sue found us the greatest apartment directly across the street from the ocean in Flagler Beach. We had a view of the water out of most of its windows. I was completely content. *I did it,* I thought. *I'm back in Florida, I came alone, I became licensed as a realtor here, and nothing is going to take me away this time.*

I turned fifty on the beach in the house we rented. I remember the morning of my birthday, I was dancing while having a cup of coffee in the enclosed Florida room, looking out at the dolphins jumping out of the water and at the fishing boats out on the horizon. What a great day that was. I always knew I would be back in Florida; I just didn't know it would take me till I was forty-nine years old to get back. Lesson to be learned: NEVER GIVE UP. If you want something badly enough, you can get it. You must just be patient.

But at times my heart was playing with my emotions. Part of me was sad for leaving my grown children and young grandchildren. I was single, I had quit my job, and I had sold my condo to move to another state. How could I have even been so strong—or so selfish, as I thought of it? Thinking back and remembering what I did, I'm surprised I actually did it. When I was in Florida, I was so happy and peaceful at first. After a few months, though, I missed the grandchildren and kids, so I would fly back to Ohio for the weekend. Then when I was back in Ohio for a couple days, I would miss Florida, so I would go back to my home on the beach. I kept going on like that for a couple of years. I felt guilty for leaving Linda, but at the same time, I wanted to have a life, too, and Ohio was not doing it for me. I fought my emotions for years, but I could not see myself living in Ohio ever again. Florida was my home. It held my heart, and I found an inner peace there.

Living on the beach, I was getting my feet wet in the real estate market and in the ocean as well. Little did I know when I became licensed that the market was about to burst. I moved there thinking I would make a good living, but the bubble busted in 2008. That was a real disappointment. There sat Sue and I, new to the area, and then the market went totally down. And I didn't know much about the area—in fact, nothing at all.

So we tried to make it work, and after about eight months of pursuing success in the real estate industry, we decided we needed to move into another direction. Sue and I decided to find jobs that would help us pay our bills. She was hired at Yellow Book first and then recruited me to the team. It was a good job. At least we had a base pay, an expense account, and commission. I decided I was not going to pursue a real estate career any longer and wanted to begin a new venture. I let my license expire, and Sue decided to put her license as inactive but keep it in case she ever wanted to get back into selling real estate.

As I look back and write this book, I feel I was like a kite: sometimes I flew with the wind. Whether this was a good quality or bad quality, I'm not sure, but after everything I had been through, nothing scared me anymore, and I wanted to try something new. As I said early in this book, my life has had many twists and turns, or *Chutes and Ladders*, as I called it, and I had learned to roll with the punches. I was like a free spirit, trying to find myself. For so many years, I had no control over my life, but at last I could call the shots and it was up to me to make it work—and I was going to make it work. I had always been controlled either by my parents, my husbands, or life's situations. I never did anything for just myself. And turning fifty really hit me. I needed to do something for me, something that made me happy. Putting my feelings on hold, I'd always tried to please others. This pinnacle birthday was like a rebirth in some odd way. Did I know what was around the next corner? No. Nor did I care at the time. I was finally on my own journey. I had to find my true self.

Living on the beach with Sue was a memory I will never forget. I lived my youth all over again, only this time I wasn't married at nineteen. We were at times crazy. When you put two women in their fifties together on the beach in a vacation environment, anything can happen. And boy, did it. We partied like rock stars. It made me chuckle: two women way past middle age acting like teenagers. Oh, there was no doubt it was a real midlife crisis for us. Yes, we were working—selling advertising for Yellow Book—and dating up a storm. There was never a dull night at our beach house. We got to the point where we would take each other on our dates just to have fun, which was crazy. Nothing serious every came out of the dates, but we did make a lot of friends.

One thing we mastered during that time was the art of entertaining. We both loved to entertain and have friends over. We constantly had guests visiting from Ohio and Canada. Linda, her husband, and her kids came to visit that summer, too, and it turned out to be a great time with them. I had only left Ohio in May, and by the time they came to visit in July, I was missing the grandchildren so much. We had so much fun during their stay, especially going to the beach every day.

We continued to live on the beach for seven months. Seven months of nothing but a dream come true for me. I had wanted that my entire life. I felt a sense of freedom, being on the ocean. Deciding to rent a home on the beach with Sue was the best decision in my life. We got along perfectly, and never once did we have a disagreement. It was like a match made in heaven. I'd never had a roommate before Sue. I had gone from living in my mother's house to living with my husband to living on my own but never sharing a home with a female friend. Sue was and still is to this day the best cook in the world, in my opinion, and I was the clean freak of the pair, so our relationship worked out great; she cooked and I cleaned. We had the time of our lives. And although we partied like old rock stars, I am not ashamed of one thing. It was the first happy time I'd had in so many years. I didn't want it to end.

The year flew by, and before I knew it we had to move because our lease was up. We next decided to rent a condo in the Palm Coast area. Moving away from Flagler Beach was probably better for us. Once you cross that bridge to enter the island and life on the beach, something magical happens to you and you lose all your good sense—trust me, that's what happened to us. It was not the best thing for residents unless they were retired or very wealthy. Sue and I seemed to be mesmerized by life at the beach and thought we had landed in paradise. I had just moved from Ohio and she had just moved from Canada, so to have that sort of lifestyle was new and exciting, especially while being single at our age. And all I will say about that is, "What happens on Flagler Beach stays on Flagler Beach."

During the year we rented the Palm Coast condo, we both grew and not just grew up but really moved into a more serious stage of life. Sue met the love of her life and after being single for over twenty years, she got married.

After our lease was up, I moved back into my parents' condo. They had already moved into a home that was being built, so the condo was just left empty. I decided to stay there for a short time alone and save some money to buy a home. I hadn't met anyone I thought would be a lifelong companion or husband, so I figured if I was to live my life alone, I should form some roots there. And buying the house was the first root I planted.

Linda had been healthy for some time with no major surgeries, but she was still taking the pain pills because she said she was in constant pain without them. Now I must admit, with everything she had been through, I couldn't imagine her being completely pain free. However, I think she took that situation to another level and knew she could convince doctors to administer pain medications based on her history. It was the first time I ever saw a person with an addiction, and in some ways, I was naïve about it. I wanted so badly to believe she was in the pain she said, but I hated seeing her when she had taken too many pills and she was high—I could see it in her eyes.

I tried to get Linda into rehab so many times. In fact, once I flew up to Ohio to watch the kids while her husband was going to take her to a rehab facility. She lasted there only two days and came home because she said she was in too much pain without the pills. Of course there would be pain, but isn't that what they call withdrawal? I was so angry that I took the next flight out of Ohio and went back to Florida. I found you cannot help someone who doesn't want help. But I was getting sucked into a vacuum of dysfunction. I kept thinking things would change.

    Over the next two years, I took many trips back and forth to see the kids and grandchildren. We were always together on holidays and Halloween. Linda had no major hospital visits for a few years, but she was becoming more and more distant. To not rock the boat, I kept my distance as well. But I knew it was only a matter of time before she would burn out. I was always worried about the kids when she drove with them in the car. But since there was nothing

I could do, I was better off living far away in Florida.

As the Christmas of 2009 came upon us, I got a phone call one day from Linda's mother-in-law. She was frantic, telling me Linda was in bed and incoherent. I immediately knew what was wrong and told her to call 911, regardless of anything Linda might say. I could tell from what she said that Linda was going into septic shock. I thought, *She must have an infection going through her body and it is reacting in this way.* As soon as I hung up the phone, I booked a flight out of Florida for that evening. In fact, I was in Ohio within seven hours.

When I got to the hospital, the doctors had already put Linda into an induced coma. She was in the Intensive Care Unit in critical condition with, as I had feared, a blood infection—septic shock—running rampant in her bloodstream, causing all her organs to shut down.

Jackie Dobrosky

As I stood in the doorway of the ICU, I felt numb. Once again I asked, "Why Linda?" She was in her thirties by then, she knew better, and if she would have caught the infection when she'd first felt it coming on, the sepsis could have been prevented. But the pills just masked all her pain. She didn't want to deal with her sickness anymore, and I think sometimes she wanted to die.

I don't know how I got the strength to watch as more bags of IV fluids were connected to her. It was December twentieth, and she was now in another very real fight for her life. If I had thought I was not going to handle her surgeries and get through them, this situation was even worse, the most serious one of all.

She was getting worse each day, and by Christmas Day, the whole family spent it in the ICU waiting room. Her sons were devastated, and they were at the age where they wanted to see their mother but were not allowed in the room. They were crying, and they went through Christmas Day eating nothing but a sandwich.

For two straight weeks, I would not leave the hospital and slept in the ICU waiting room. Linda's mother-in-law took care of the kids, but I noticed Linda's husband was not really involved with their care or Linda's traumatic situation. He just went to work as usual and would come to the hospital in the evenings for an hour or two. He never stayed in Linda's room very long, and when the doctors would come out to the waiting room, it was Linda's father and I who would jump up and get an update; Robert would just sit there playing a video game on his phone, and I found his behavior so very strange. But I didn't have time or the energy to worry about him. I realized he had it easy with his mother taking care of his children and me taking care of his wife. He was all alone in his own world, and call it a gut feeling, but I knew something was up. I just couldn't put my finger on it.

Jackie Dobrosky

Well, as I said, Christmas came and went. The kids would visit the hospital every other day, weather permitting, and it was a rough winter that year. The kids never had a chance to open their presents. They wanted to wait for their mother to get better, and they were too young to realize their mother may not be coming home. It was heart wrenching the day they sang a holiday song, I think it was "Jingle Bells," and recorded it for me to take to their mother and let her hear it. They said it would make her smile and get better. I played that in her ear time and time again. What I found out through her nurses was that a comatose person may still be able to hear you even though they can't communicate. The nurse told me never to cry in the room as Linda would hear it. So instead, I talked to her, braided her hair, painted her nails, played the Christmas carols for her that the kids had recorded every day. I kept telling her, "Come back, come back, Linda. The boys need you." We had a priest come in and pray over her. My son even brought some special rosary beads he had and draped them over her bed. All we had was God and God's will.

New Year's Eve was fast approaching and still no improvement. Two other men died of septic shock in the ICU unit during that week. I was frightened and frantic. "God, I can't do this. I can't lose her. She has two small boys!" I cried. She also had a husband who wasn't worth a dime, in my opinion, and who could not have cared less whether she lived or died.

On New Year's Eve, my ex-husband and I spent the holiday in the waiting room with along with my sister Judy. The next day, the family came to the hospital and my brokers from the company I'd worked for while I was an agent in Ohio had a catered dinner sent to us there. I couldn't believe the love that poured out from them as well as other friends and family.

Yet during all of that, Robert was nowhere to be found. My son felt something strange was going on, so one morning after New Year's Day he showed up unannounced at Linda's house. With his own key to her house, Joe walked in to find Robert sleeping with his sister-in-law, right in my daughter's bed. That did not go over very well, to say the least. There was his wife in the hospital, possibly dying, while he was sleeping with his brother's wife. I could barely comprehend it when my son told me.

Even after being caught, Robert still didn't appear at the hospital, and by that time, Linda's dad and I were not going to address the situation because we had just been informed Linda was not going to make it. Her lungs had collapsed, and her kidneys were failing. They told us we should start planning for her passing. I broke down, both emotionally and physically. "This is not supposed to happen. I am the one who should die first," I cried. If it weren't for my sister Judy, I would not have made it. She was there every day and never left my side. I only left the hospital for a short while every other day to shower and return as quickly as I could. I sat like a statue. I had no feeling. I felt like I couldn't breathe. I couldn't drink water. I got to the point where I couldn't even cry. I felt like I'd died. I walked into Linda's room one day, seeing the machines still keeping her alive, and I sat down and cried. I didn't care what the nurses said. I wanted Linda to know I was crying.

"Get up!" I screamed. "Linda, get up! You can't leave," I said while tears ran uncontrollably down my face. Then the nurses told me I had to leave, that I was out of control. *Out of control?* I thought. *How would you react if you were faced with this situation? I've had very little sleep in the past two weeks, enough food to keep only a bird alive, and you're telling me I am out of control? Ok, maybe I am. What do I do?*

I went to the hospital chapel to pray. "Help me, God. Why are we going through this?" I prayed so long I fell asleep in a pew and woke up hours later. I felt that the biblical Job had it easier, that I was being tested way beyond anything I could possibly handle. My daughter was dying, her husband was having an affair, and I had two small grandsons who were heartbroken about their mother.

To my surprise as I walked back to the ICU, I was told that Linda was responding and they were slowly pulling her off life support and that she was starting to breathe on her own. I almost fell to the ground. "Lord, you have not forsaken us," I cried. I walked into Linda's room to see she was sitting up and off the respirator. All the nurses were crying. Linda's improvement was a Christmas miracle. It was a joyous holiday after all the stress and sadness we had endured those past weeks.

Once she was really awake and talking, Linda couldn't understand what had happened. We told her she had contracted a blood infection that turned into septic shock and that they had put her into an induced coma till they could effectively treat the infection. She didn't remember anything about it. And although she was released from the ICU within a few days, she was kept in the hospital for some time. After another week or so she would be able to come home.

Now came the part I dreaded to tell her: that her husband was having an affair with his brother's wife, Molly. To complicate things further, Molly was also Linda's best friend.

When my son finally broke the news to Linda, she did not believe him. It was a mess. She claimed Joe was just trying to start trouble between her and her husband. I tried to explain to Linda that her husband had hardly visited her while she was in the coma, that it was her father and I who slept in the waiting room every night on sofas and lounge chairs; Robert never spent one night even though he was "kids free" because his mother was watching the children.

As Linda refused to believe the truth, it was like watching myself all over again. I remember when my parents came to me and told me my husband was having an affair and I didn't believe them. I thought they were just trying to split us up. Then, twenty-one years later, my daughter was being told the same thing about her sister-in-law and husband, and she doesn't believe us. Déjà vu.

It was the second week in January when Linda finally came home from the hospital. We celebrated Christmas with the kids, they opened their presents, and it appeared everyone was happy. Since I had taken a month off work, I needed to get back to Florida after Linda was settled in. But then came the amazing part. She moved her sister in law into the house to take care of her. The same woman her husband was having an affair with. Okay, I just couldn't do crazy anymore. I don't know if something happened when she was in the coma and she lost part of her mind or memory or if she was in total denial. But I couldn't take another minute of it and I left.

As I was flying back to Florida, I thought back on the whole month. *How could this keep happening? How is it possible? Why does this never end and only get more dysfunctional? I don't want to be part of it. If she is going to have this woman and her kids living in her house, then so be it. I stayed during the time I was needed. She will have to work this one out alone.*

And it didn't take long, not long at all. You see, while Linda was in the coma, it gave her a chance to go through detox. She was no longer addicted to the opioids. And as the days went by and her mind became clearer, it finally hit her as to what was going on right under her own roof, and let's just say all heck broke out. She confronted Molly about the affair, and Molly didn't deny it. In fact, Linda beat her up. Yes, a woman in a wheelchair beat Molly up and cornered her in her bedroom. Robert came to

Molly's rescue and told Linda he was leaving her for Molly, and they packed their clothes and left—Robert, Molly, and Molly's two small children. Linda freaked out and called her brother, who ran to her side to do all he could to console her, but he was the one who had told her what was going on while she was in the hospital.

I was already back in Florida when all this happened, so there was not much I could do at that point. Instead, Linda's dad and her brother stayed with her for a few days. She still needed to be looked after. My suggestion before I left to go back to Florida had been to get home health care to come to the house. Her insurance would pay for it, and they would stay and take shifts. But Linda refused, so with me being back in Florida, there was nothing I could do for her then.

Months went by, and I received a call from Linda, who told me she had acquired a large bedsore when she was in the coma. It was burying into her buttocks. Doctors told her it would have to heal from the inside out as it was very deep. I had been through that type of healing process with her over the years so many times I could have handled it with my eyes closed, but I couldn't leave Florida. I was in the process of buying a new home. As an alternative, I suggested she come to Florida, where I would take care of her while she healed. I sent her a ticket in hopes she would come and have some rest and get her head together after everything that just took place. I, on the other hand, was next moving into my new home and doing some renovations.

Linda was now off painkillers completely, and she was very clear in her thoughts. After she found her mother-in-law would help with the kids, she came to Florida and was with me for about a week, during which time her wound began to progressively heal. One day, Linda had the idea she wanted her kids and couldn't stay here without them. They were out on spring break, but I really wasn't that thrilled with her idea. I had so much to do already with working a job, moving and unpacking and renovating my new home, and taking care of Linda's wound. I started to wonder, *When does this end? Now she wants me to bring the kids.*

So what did I do? I brought the kids.

Little did I know that as soon as I brought the kids to Florida, Linda would decide she wanted to go back to Ohio. She was getting together with a young man, Chris, who had worked for her and Robert's company. Years before, she'd had a little flirtation with him and thought she would get Robert jealous. So she tracked him down, found out he was still single, and plotted to meet him in order to get even with Molly and Robert. She claimed she wanted to go back to Ohio just to straighten out a few things and would then be back in a couple of days.

My Unexpected Journey

How stupid was I to have paid for that whole crazy situation? Now I knew I was codependent, that she was my Achilles' heel. Why was I doing that to myself?

As she left to go back to Ohio, I had the kids while my house was being torn apart—I was having ceramic tile put in the whole house, so that meant all my furniture was in the garage. I took the two boys to the family condo, which was empty and we stayed there for a week. Easter was fast approaching, so we colored Easter eggs and I took the boys on an Easter-egg hunt.

At that point, there was no sign of Linda returning to Florida or of her asking for the boys back. I finally found out through my son that my daughter had gone back with a vengeance to get even with her husband and had hooked up with Chris. Well, during the short time she was back in town, she managed to cause quite a stir. A very large fight broke out at her house between Chris and Robert, and there were fights, bloodshed, police involved, and two people arrested. All along, I didn't know anything about what was happening until afterward.

Well, after that all took place, I decided I'd had enough. I wasn't going to be a babysitter while Linda was up in Ohio playing her get-even game with some guy. I sent the kids back and knew that what I couldn't change I must let go. It was Easter, for goodness' sake! The boys should be with their parents. Hadn't these children been through enough? As much as I did not want to send them back, I did.

The next couple of months were destructive, and everything went crazy. Linda and Robert, it turned out, were involved in illegal things to make money. I felt like I was watching my own younger life all over again. She was following in my footsteps. *What happened? Where did things go wrong?* Linda was afraid Robert would steal the kids from her, so she wanted to move to Florida to start a new life, and she did it with Chris. She claimed she loved him, but how could that be? She had just been in a coma less than a year earlier. Doesn't this sound like an old record, already? It appears everyone in my family heads south when things get too out of hand.

Even though I was a thousand miles away from all that was happening in Ohio, it then became my problem to solve. So what did I do? I paid for Linda to move to Florida, rented her a truck, and found her an apartment in Palm Coast. And along with her, she brought Chris into her life and our family. Once they arrived, I help them get set up. I guess I was looking at the bright side; I had my grandsons close by at last. My heart was complete. And no more trips back to Ohio. I figured if my son wanted to see us, I would buy him a ticket to come to Florida. I was done with Ohio once and for all.

Jackie Dobrosky

Linda, Chris, and the boys were getting settled into their first of three apartments they had in the three years they lived together—yes, I said *three*. It was just short of mayhem. They were evicted from each apartment. Each time I was called for help, and each time I ran. I knew at that point I was a true codependent with Linda. I knew it was wrong, but I could not help myself. I kept thinking of the children, and I felt it was my responsibility to protect them.

I was getting more and more disgusted with Linda's life choices. But every time I would bring it up, she would cry about losing her leg and then I would feel guilty. I don't know why I kept reacting like that, but back then, she knew just what buttons to push to make me jump. I was addicted to that crazy dysfunction and at the same time didn't want anything to do with it. My stepdad set her up in a new business here in Florida and tried to help her and Chris get back on their feet.

In the span of three years, however, the business was destroyed again—the second business to go down the tubes. After the fourth move she and Chris made while they were together, their relationship fizzled and they broke up.

Linda moved back to Ohio after that to try and co-parent with her ex-husband, who was still with his brother's wife. It was a horrible year for Linda: she couldn't make it on her own, and Robert didn't help with a penny. I ended up sending money to help keep her utilities connected. I even flew up there one time to buy her a van. Now, I know as you read this you are thinking I am part of the problem. And yes, if Dr. Phil heard my story, he would probably have suggested mental health counseling for me and I knew it. It was going on twenty-eight years of living to keep Linda alive, and I had become her punching bag. At that point, I decided I needed help and I was not to ashamed to ask for it. How much could one person go through? And that time, I was talking about getting the help for myself. So yes, I started counseling and thought I was making progress.

After many months, the counselor did tell me I suffered from post-traumatic stress disorder (PTSD) from being a caregiver involved with such a devastating sickness and lifestyle. And she also said I was a textbook codependent. *Oh great,* I thought. *I have become a nut case, and all in the name of keeping my daughter healthy and safe.*

One thing I learned is that first I must take care of myself before I can take care of anyone else. That thought had never entered my head. I thought that would be selfish. But look where doing it my way landed me—not in a place I would recommend for anyone. I am proud to be writing this today to say, "I am not perfect." I have made many mistakes, but today I call them "learned lessons." I had to distinguish between guilt and truth. I had to rebuild my strength and confidence.

And after so many years of beating myself up, I learned through deep therapy that I had nothing to feel guilty about. Linda was born with a congenital tumor disease, yet I felt guilty for so long that she had contracted it and felt it was my fault. Doctors didn't know where it came from; it was a very rare tumor. And I did all I could to help and to get her the medical help she needed. It was not my fault that after the third time the tumor came back it was misdiagnosed. But all that kept ringing through my mind was Linda blaming me for her amputation and resenting me so much. I realized that the compensation I was giving to her was to ease my own feelings, though, and not hers. Guilt is a very bad thing to live with and an even worse one to let go of because sometimes it's embedded in the mind so deeply we can't realize our worst enemy is the guilt itself.

CHAPTER 8

During the year Linda went back to Ohio, I decided to sell my house in Palm Coast, and I had the opportunity to buy an investment home from my parents. It was a much larger home than I would have needed, but the terms were great and I loved the house and its location. I sold my house for a nice-sized profit and moved forward, keeping busy with work and trying to take the Linda obsession out of my head; I didn't want it to consume me for the rest of my life. I was now learning to have a life, to feel happy for each day, because we are never guaranteed another day. "The Serenity Prayer" rather than guilt became embedded in my mind: "God, grant me the serenity to accept the things I cannot change, the courage to change the things I can, and the wisdom to know the difference."

I wasn't perfect but was getting better every day. I prayed for the strength to overcome my so-called addiction to control the things I had no control over. I knew I had done my best with Linda and the children; now I tried to release and give them back to God.

Also within that year Linda and the boys were gone, I met my third husband. It was really an unexpected meeting because this time I wasn't running away from anything. This time I wasn't needy or lacking attention. This time I was becoming a strong, independent woman because of all my trials and misgivings. I could take care of myself, I was not lonely, and I was pretty happy living alone. It was approaching ten years since my last divorce, and I was so used to living alone that as those years flew quickly by, I didn't give much thought to having a serious relationship. I'd had a series of short-term relationships that never seemed to last more than a few months, and as a woman reaching my mid-fifties, having a longer one was not a main priority for me—until my friend Sue asked me when I was going to settle down.

To help me do just that, she decided to go online and find a husband for me. It started out as a joke, but she found a man online with the best bio I'd ever read. Then she decided to send him a message and sign my name to it.

Days later, I received a letter back from the man, whose name was Jim. He was very polite and interesting. After texting a few times, we spoke on the phone and then we decided to meet for a short lunch. It was a very pleasant lunch, and he was an intelligent man and I could tell he had integrity. It wasn't love at first sight, but then again, I was approaching our date in a totally different way. It didn't have to be the Fourth-of-July fireworks; that's what had gotten me in trouble in the past. Instead, I wanted substance and friendship first. I liked his company, and we started to see each other just for dinners and maybe a movie. We kept our friendship a secret from most everyone we knew. I guess you could say we wanted to get to know each other first before we introduced each other's family and friends into our lives.

Our friendship started in the early spring, and it wasn't until I was leaving to go to Ohio to spend the Christmas holiday of 2013 with my children and grandchildren that I realized he was getting very serious. So much, in fact, that the night before I left for my trip he asked me to marry him. I was totally taken by surprise and overcome. I said, "Yes," and not because I felt time was running out for me to find a life partner. I really did love him—and I *liked* him, which was something I couldn't say about the other med I'd dated. When I went to Ohio, though, I never mentioned to anyone I was even dating someone let alone planning on getting married.

The trip started out well but ended up less than that. Linda was getting sick again, and I knew it was from lack of her taking care of herself. I arrived four days before Christmas Eve, and by the day before Christmas Eve she was admitted into the hospital with respiratory problems. Infection had set into her lungs, and the physicians were concerned it would become more serious if not treated immediately with IV antibiotics. For me, it was reminiscent of the other Christmases Linda had spent in the hospital.

At that point, I didn't know what to do with the kids, since their father was worthless as far as being of any help with them. I was all alone, so I decided to take the boys to an afternoon movie. How weird was that? I was sitting in a theater with about thirty other people who, I assumed, had no families. It all felt so abnormal to me. Since I became a mother many years ago, Christmas Eve had always been the holiday celebration I hosted, and now here we sat, my two grandsons and I, in an afternoon matinee theater, watching a movie.

After the matinee, we decide to go to Walmart and shop for Christmas dinner. How weird it all continued to feel. And let me just say that being in Walmart on Christmas Eve was like a total nightmare. I shopped for Christmas dinner like a zombie. The boys were very sad and angry at that point, so they started to fight with each other in the store. I wanted to just disappear into thin air.

By the time we got home and had unpacked our groceries, it was late and the kids were getting ready for bed. As I put the groceries away, I wondered what was going to happen to Linda. I couldn't be in two places at one time, and right then the kids needed me more than she did. I knew she was being well taken care of.

With their presents under the tree, I didn't know how to comfort the two boys who were lying in bed, crying again about their mother being in the hospital. So, we just prayed together and asked God to make Linda better and let her come home and spend Christmas with us. I then went back into the living room, fell into a chair, and cried. Another Christmas, another sickness, and I felt so helpless. The next thing I remember was waking up and it was morning. Instead of the kids waking up and running to the tree, they were still sleeping. I think their joy was taken away. I checked on them and then shut their door to let them sleep before making a cup of coffee and sitting at the kitchen table. Numbly, I thought to myself, *Merry Christmas*, as I took a sip of coffee and looked out the window to watch the snow come down.

A little while later, I heard the rustling of the boys waking up. I started to drift off in my mind as I was thinking, *What do I say to them?* I had already called the hospital and spoken with Linda, but she wasn't sure what they were going to do or if they would release her that day. I was angry with her at that point. Because she had been abusing her body for years, she was getting more infections and her diabetes was getting worse. She was a horrible diabetic and I couldn't change a thing about it. She was on her own journey, one that was detrimentally affecting two small boys. They didn't deserve that by any means. Their father didn't want anything to do with them, and their mother was not stepping up to the plate and being a responsible parent.

Linda's and my relationship had been tainted for years by then. Before she had left Florida the last time, the boys lived with me alone for a whole school year while she was "getting herself together." Linda was taking pills again and I had taken the boys away from her. She was still living with Chris before the move back to Ohio. And the real reason she went back to Ohio was because I couldn't and wouldn't put up with her dysfunctional lifestyle. I didn't deserve it. She said she was going to co-parent with her ex, but that turned out to be a joke. Yes, she was a sick woman and life had not always been fair to her, but these two boys never asked to be born. With their father out of the picture, it was time Linda decided to get herself together, mentally and physically, and be the best she could.

I had done the best I could for her, but I wasn't a magician, just her mother, and now she had to be the best mother to her boys. She had all the resources at hand, but her choices put her in places that were less than acceptable. I always stepped in and made sure the boys got anything they needed.

Just at that moment, I snapped out of my unpleasant thoughts. The kids were walking into the kitchen as my mind came back to reality and out of the fog I was just in. "Grandma, is Mommy coming home today?" they both asked me at once. Holding back tears, I said I wasn't sure. I told them as soon as we got dressed and I put our Christmas ham in the oven, we would take a ride to the hospital to see her. They both ran to the shower, fighting to get in first.

I looked up at the ceiling as I prayed for the strength to get through that situation again. "Please, Lord, give me the strength to pull this off. I am breaking down." I was angry, not at God, but at the situation. All I kept thinking was: *Here we go again—another Christmas, another hospital.*

We arrived at the hospital around eleven o'clock that very cold, snowy Christmas morning. I had not driven in snow for years, so I drove slowly and carefully while the kids, anxious to get to the hospital, kept coaxing me to go faster, which I didn't do. I wasn't about to have an accident on my way to the hospital on Christmas. When we arrived, it evoked such an odd feeling, with the hospital full of holiday decorations and even Christmas trees. There were very few people in the hallways, and I still remember the smell of the hospital. It especially brought back the memories of the Christmas we had spent in the hospital when Linda was in the coma with septic shock.

As I held both boys' hands, we walked down the hallway in silence to her room. We found her sitting up in bed, and the boys ran over to give her a kiss. I stood there totally numb. It was all I could do to bend down and give her a kiss. I was so disappointed in her; knowing it was her lack of care for herself that had landed her there. I was tired of trying to fix someone who didn't want to fix herself. She was all smiles and said the doctor was just in and had released her to go home. Great. I didn't even know what was wrong with her. She hadn't even asked why she couldn't breathe and why her sugar levels were so high. All she wanted to do was go home.

So, I did exactly that—I took her home. I never asked another question. If she didn't care, why should I? It was getting way beyond crazy. As we arrived home, the boys excitedly opened their presents and gave their mother her gifts. I just went straight to the kitchen to check on dinner and continue preparing our Christmas meal. The day went on, and we ate dinner around five o'clock. Later, her father came over and her brother visited. I went through the motions of the day, lifeless. The joy was taken out of me. I was just doing what I do.

I went back to Florida a few days later, but I never said a word to anyone in Ohio about my new relationship and my upcoming marriage. For starters, the timing was not right, and secondly, I didn't want to share my news yet.

My arrival back in Florida should have been a joyous occasion but was instead tainted with depression and sadness. I tried my best to hide it from Jim, but he was way too wise and saw right through me. I dodged many questions he tried to ask about how the holiday had gone. The one thing I love most about him was he didn't pressure me. He dropped it; he knew something was wrong, but he allowed me my privacy and figured I would share it when I felt the time was right. New Year's Eve was just days away when he surprised me with a wonderful night. We went on a cruise ship that traveled out just a little from the coastline and we rang in the new year, gambling and dancing on a wonderful ship with a couple thousand people. That was a wonderful time after the Christmas I had just experienced.

Now that the new year, 2014, had begun, we decided to make plans to get married. I didn't want a long, drawn-out engagement, and at our ages, with me being fifty-seven and him being sixty-four at the time, we decided to plan it soon. I wasn't going to live with him without marriage. So, we decided to marry on February 1, 2014, just one month after the first of the year. I still hadn't told my kids about my upcoming marriage, and I don't know why. I guess I still felt the timing was not right, or maybe after two failed marriages, they might not have had faith that I would make the right decision, and I wasn't willing to be judged. I was going down this road on my own, without anyone's opinion, and I did just that. In the end, the only others involved in our wedding were my best friend, Sue, and her husband, Jim, who stood up for us.

We had a magical wedding. We rented a limo from a company that also would conduct the ceremony itself, and we rented a castle on the beach as our venue. Yes, it was a real castle, and I felt like a princess. The limo brought us to the castle and then rolled out the red carpet as the gate to the abbey (castle) opened and we entered, followed by Sue and Jim. I'd always wanted to feel like a princess, and that day I had my chance, in a castle with my soul mate. It took three tries, but I felt this time I felt I'd finally gotten it right. From inside and outside, I was finally marrying for the right reason. After the ceremony, the man who had built the castle in Vilano Beach, Florida, took us on a tour through the amazing structure. I couldn't believe I had pulled it off with no one knowing I was getting married. It was very empowering.

It wasn't until we returned to the limo and Sue started taking pictures of us after the wedding and putting it on social media that my kids started calling me on the phone, freaking out. *Gotcha!* I thought. I was now my own woman and did what I wanted, so they'd just have to get over it. My son wished me the best of everything, but Linda was angry I hadn't told her. *Oh well,* I thought. *She will get over it.* I wasn't letting that ruin my wedding night.

The limo drove us around St. Augustine, the oldest city in the United

States. It was still all lit up from the Christmas holidays, and the historic town was stunning. We had dinner at a wonderful restaurant on that special night, the start of a whole new life. I had been single for over ten years. I was now a married woman with a husband.

After we got back from our wedding, we decided to have a little party at our home for a few friends and family to celebrate our new marriage. It took place on February fifteenth, and I had a Valentine theme for the occasion. Only our closest friends and family were invited, and we had a fabulous time. My stepdad, who I never really thought of as my *step*father, gave a speech and toast that night. He said he wished us well and that he felt after many attempts I'd finally gotten it right with my new husband. Everyone toasted, and we all smiled. I kissed him and thanked him for those kind words.

Soon after, on February twenty-fifth, my husband, Jim, had knee-replacement surgery. I wasn't crazy about once again going through the whole hospital and recuperation process and taking care of a sick person. I was tainted from all the years I'd had to live in hospitals and take care of Linda. I had a stigma in my mind of illness, but hey, I could handle anything, right? And we got through that. I went back to work, and the month flew by.

Before I knew it, March had arrived and Jim was beginning to get back on his feet. I hadn't heard much from Linda, which was okay with me. I needed a break for a while. Between taking care of my new husband and working, I felt like I was on a hamster wheel.

CHAPTER 9

In the meantime, an unexpected tragedy happened in my life. My stepdad died in a very tragic plane crash on March twenty-first, just a month after I was married. Although my stepdad was an excellent pilot and had his own plane, on that day he was unfortunately not flying it. Instead, he was in a friend's plane, teaching him how to execute specific types of landings when the accident happened. My stepdad died on the spot, but his friend walked away. Well, this was way beyond devastating for all of us. Dad was the pillar of our family. What were we going to do now? My mother, in all the years since they were married, never knew how to take care of herself—he did everything for her. He treated her like a queen, and she'd loved every minute of it. He was her rock; he was our rock; he was the glue that held our family together throughout all the trials we had. We always knew we could go to Dad and he would have the answers. But now he was gone, and the family would never be the same again.

Dad was buried in a military ceremony, and it was done beautifully. So many people came to celebrate his life with our family. But in the end, the finality hit us. Dad was gone; he would never be back. It took a toll on the whole family. After Dad died, the family seemed to split up. The family we once had and knew was no longer. It was a whole new normal life for us to get used to living. My mother was faced with so much after his death, and it took years to settle a lot of his business matters.

My Unexpected Journey

The only family left for her was my sister Judy and me. The other three kids had moved far away. The family was an emotional mess. Dad had been everyone's strength, and now God had taken him home.

The next couple of months became a total blur to me. Between my sister and me helping my mother with her personal business and being there for her emotionally, we were drained. My mother didn't even know how to pay her own bills. My dad was a very successful businessman at the time of his passing, and my mother had many loose ends to straighten up with the businesses he'd owned. They also owned multiple homes, two boats, two airplanes—all things that needed to be addressed. The fact that my stepfather was a self-made man when he passed only brought out one thing in many people: greed. My half sister inherited a massive amount of wealth from life-insurance policies my mother knew nothing about, took the money, and left town immediately and has not been seen for the last three-and-a-half years. One of my sisters, who lives in California and who has mental health and substance abuse issues, emotionally flew the coop. No one else stuck it out with my mother but my sister Judy and me. I never dreamed that when Dad died the family could be broken so fast over greed and money, neither of which had I grown up with.

I had only been married for one month, my husband was recuperating from a knee replacement, my dad just died tragically, and my daughter was having more financial problems in Ohio and was starting to sell her furniture just to live. I could have had a breakdown had I allowed myself. But for some reason, that thought never came into my head. I was in survival mode. I learned to work best under the worst stress. I am not sure if that is a gift or not, but it kept me sane. I took things one at a time. Thankfully, Jim was getting better from his knee surgery. It was now going on three months and he could get back to work.

But it was my mother who was having the worst time of all. I was so worried something was going to happen to her. She was so dependent on my dad, and now she was all alone. With the grace of God, we all got through it, and let me just say it was not easy.

As the months flew by, things were getting worse with Linda and her living arrangements in Ohio, and she wanted to come back to Florida. She couldn't see how her life would work in Ohio. So Jim and I decided to put together an apartment for her here in Florida. With the help of the used-furniture stores and consignment shops, we furnished an apartment for her and the boys. It was beautiful and completely set up with everything they would need.

Linda had already sold everything she had in Ohio and was ready for the move, with suitcases waiting. Jim rented a van, and we left on a Friday afternoon to go and get her, the boys, and their belongings.

Jackie Dobrosky

After fifteen hours of straight driving to arrive at their door, we picked them up and went directly to a hotel, where we all slept for the night before taking off the following day to head back to Florida. We drove straight through again and got back late on Sunday evening. When we arrived at their new apartment and began to get them settled, their eyes showed total shock. It was truly turn-key, ready to live in. It even had food in the refrigerator. They loved it, and I think they were all very happy with it.

We were back at home, and to say we were tired was mild as I awoke that Monday morning. As I drank my cup of coffee, I thought about how surprising it was that Jim and I were able to accomplish so much in a two-and-a-half-day trip. I heard the shower running, so I knew he was getting ready for work. This man was my angel. God had to have sent him to me. I couldn't have done all of that alone. He came into the kitchen, bright eyed and ready to go to work. I had made some breakfast and already packed his lunch. We didn't say much to each other about the weekend. He just smiled at me, gave me a kiss, and went off to work.

Between taking care of my mother and making sure Linda and the boys were okay in their own life, I was letting my business go, a little at a time. I know that was wrong, but I didn't have it in me to continue to build the small business I had started. God was leading me toward a different direction in my life, and it wasn't my job. Since I was married now and Jim was working, I could take the time to reconsider where I was going. Until then, I was with my mother daily. She was not a well woman and hadn't been for many years. She'd always had problems with her back, and Dad had passed while she had still been recovering from her last back surgery. Judy and I tried to take care of her as best we could.

Now came another twist and unexpected problem: Linda was

experiencing major pain in her good leg, which had been operated on years before. She could not bend it, and every time she stood up, the pain was excruciating. We decided to get her to the Mayo Clinic at that point. Rather than consulting any local doctors, I wanted to find out from the big guys right up front.

Well, they couldn't help her, but they did send us to a doctor in Orlando who dealt with very serious knee problems. We went to see him, and after a few tests, he decided to open the knee and take out the hardware they had installed years prior. *Does this ever end?* I thought. More surgeries, my mother in dire need, I was newly married, and I needed to find a job. I thought for sure I was going to break down. Then I remembered my prayer to God: "Lord, give me strength to handle anything you give me," I prayed nightly. And that's exactly what He gave me. I was stronger than I could ever imagine and did not have time to question or to feel sorry for myself. I felt like I was on a mission.

First and foremost, Linda did get her surgery, and Jim watched the boys while I went to Orlando to be with her. She only stayed overnight and then we came home. She and the boys stayed with us for the next week. School had not yet started, so the kids were able to swim every day in our pool and hang out while their mom healed. I bounced back and forth to and from my mother's house and did the best I could to help and relieve my sister. Judy was running a business at the time and was totally stressed. Each of us was just trying to do the best we could each day. We had no control of anything. We just had to do our best with what we had at the time.

Before I knew it, school was starting for the kids, but Linda's health was not good. She was now getting older. She was worn down from years of sickness, multiple surgeries, and her abuse of the pain medications. In the months following, she found out she had cirrhosis of the liver, and she never drank liquor. I found out that there were other ways to contract cirrhosis and that hers was from years of taking pain medicine. Linda never seemed to recover from the knee pain even after they removed the hardware. Her pain was constant, and the doctors eventually sent her to a pain clinic to manage the pain. That is not a good thing for a person who has had a problem with opioid addiction in the past. It was like putting a bandage on a wound that couldn't heal. All it did was cover the problem, not resolve it. After months that year, the doctor from Orlando said she would not be a candidate for a knee replacement, so we wondered what to do next.

We began the new school year with trips to a specialist at the Mayo Clinic to treat the cirrhosis, but the problem was that it couldn't be treated until Linda stopped the one thing that was aggravating it: the pain medications. It became a vicious cycle, her pain and the pills. She was also not keeping her diabetes under control. And a few times that year, her sugar levels got so high we had to rush her to the hospital in an ambulance. And more than a few times, I was scared out of my mind she was going into a diabetic coma. We went back and forth, back and forth. It was like a sick game. It now was apparent to me that she was never going to get well; she was way past getting help. First, she had to take her diabetes seriously, and for so many years she hadn't. Now with all the insulin shots, her glucose levels still fluctuated back and forth, high and low. I couldn't even get her to lay off the soda. Diet or regular, it was all bad for her. I couldn't get her to realize how important her diet was, and when she missed meals, it hurt her. She didn't care. I saw nothing more than a downward spiral, something I knew I could not fix. Thank God I was still in counseling. My therapist was my saving grace. Had it not been for her keeping me in check, I would not be writing this book to share my most intimate stories.

The year continued to fly by, and it was filled with sickness and pain, both for Linda and then my mother, who looked to be facing yet another back surgery. I might as well have forgotten about my own life and my marriage. I had no life. I ate and slept to take care of both my mother and Linda.

It was just after Christmas that year that my husband said to me, "Why don't you take your family on a cruise to celebrate Linda's tenuous life? Not a good-bye cruise, but a celebration of life. And bring the whole family on the cruise."

I thought hard and long about it. That sounded very good to me. I thought we should do something to make all of us smile and be happy for one special week we would never forget. With Linda's health not getting better, I didn't see a silver lining in her future. I planned a celebration of life.

My Unexpected Journey

I booked the cruise for the day after the kids got out of school. My husband did not want to go; he wanted me to have that special time with my family, so I did it. I made reservations for myself, Linda, the boys, my son, my mother, and my nephew. It gave us something to look forward to, something positive for a change. We had experienced so much unhappiness, sickness, surgery, and near-death episodes with Linda, and then there were my mother's failing health, her surgeries, and the tragic death of my dad in a plane crash. Heck, we all deserved to get away.

I booked the best-of-the-best room for Linda and me. It was a massive suite with a living area and a large deck to sit on. It was like an apartment. I wanted her to have a room she could get around in with her wheelchair without difficulty. The boys shared a cabin across from us, and Mitchel, my nephew, had his own room next to the kids'. Joe had his own cabin near my mother's suite. We were all on the same level, which was perfect. We went to the western Caribbean. I gave each person a credit card to do with and spend on whatever they wanted on the ship. Crazy? Yes, but I didn't care. Remember, it was the trip of a lifetime. In addition, at each port we visited, they had the opportunity to do any excursion they wanted. To begin with, I went everywhere my son went. Whatever he did, I booked also for myself. Crazy in every way. I was on that cruise to let loose. We rented scooters in the Bahamas. We rented jet skis in St. Thomas, and I had never been on one before. The boys loved it. What a rush we all experienced.

The last adventurous excursion was to zip line in Puerto Rico. Zip lining had always been on my bucket list as one of my thrill-seeking adventures. Joe and my nephew wanted to go as well. As the bus trucked its way up a large mountain, I sat there in such excitement. I was a mother and grandmother closing in on my sixties, and I was going on an experience to zip line in an area I wasn't familiar with. I was so compelled to do it, I had to do it, and nothing was going to stop me from fulfilling my bucket-list wish. When we arrived, however, the man in charge of the zip line told me I could not go because I was wearing sandals and you couldn't do it with open-toed footwear. I pitched a fit. I was determined to go on the zip line no matter what. Joe asked if they had any cardboard and duct tape, and believe it or not, he duct-taped my toes in my shoes and I went on the zip line. It was the most terrifying experience of my life, I hated every minute, it was scary beyond anything I had ever done, and I ended up breaking the fibula bone in my left leg.

I wasn't aware I had fractured the leg until we returned from the trip. After noticing I couldn't walk and the pain was so bad, I went to my orthopedic doctor at the Mayo Clinic and he said I needed surgery. I was on a scooter for three months because I could not put any weight on the leg. Now here's where the story has its major twist. One day soon after my surgery, Linda had to spend a day at Mayo, seeing her doctors. Since I couldn't drive, Jim drove Linda and me to the facility. I wanted to hear firsthand what was going on with Linda's health, even though I was in a cast and on a scooter. Jim pushed Linda to her appointments and I just scooted around, trying to catch up.

It wasn't until we stopped to have lunch that fateful afternoon at the Mayo Clinic that I discovered I could not eat or even drink water. Something was wrong. It felt like my throat was closing or like something was stuck in it. I didn't know what was happening. So after Linda's last appointment that day, my husband demanded we go to the emergency department and get the problem checked out. We must have made quite a picture, with Linda in her wheelchair and me on my scooter. The ER didn't know who the patient was at first, but they soon found out and I was whisked away to have a CAT (computerized axial tomography) scan done on my chest. The results were something I never thought I would hear: "The CAT scan revealed an aneurysm in your aorta." *HUH?* I thought. *What does that mean?*

All that would register in my mind was that something serious was going on in my heart.

After what seemed like hours, the attending doctor decided to admit me that same night. The plan was to run some more intensive tests the following day. I was scared. *What do they have to do to fix me? I can't be sick. I have to take care of the family.* I was supposed to be the rock after Dad died. How could I be ill? So many thoughts raced through my mind. I was so anxious the nurses finally had to give me something to calm me down. *Am I dying? Do I have heart failure?* You just can't imagine all the crazy thoughts going through this mind of mine. I didn't feel sick. I thought maybe it was just a mistake or better yet, a nightmare. Finally, the sedative kicked in and I fell asleep.

It wasn't until the next morning that the doctors came into my room and told me their plans for my testing. First, they would do a catheterization to see if I had blockage in the heart. I was taken in the same day and put under anesthetic. When I returned to my room, Jim was waiting so patiently, but he looked scared and drained. The test proved that I did indeed have a large aneurysm in my aorta in the heart and I had a defective valve that would have to be replaced. I needed to have open-heart surgery to fix the problems. And the kicker to everything? They couldn't operate on me because I had the cast on my leg. I had to go home and wait for the leg to heal first. *Oh, that's just great,* I thought. *How can I go home, knowing this aneurysm could blow at any time?* And the doctors were sending me home and telling me to just live life normally, which made no sense in my mind.

My Unexpected Journey

When I got home, I was afraid to move. I just sat on the sofa and crossed my arms, with tears welling up in my eyes. I was afraid to even go to the bathroom because I knew I had to use the scooter and was afraid it would cause the aneurysm to grow or burst. I was even terrified to sleep, because I thought I wouldn't wake up. Fear consumed me. I was mentally out of control, and I knew I had to get a grip on myself or I could make it worse. Finally, when I came to my senses, I took a step back and realized that the one and only person who could help me was the Lord. Fear was my enemy. God was in control of my life. He had always been there for me in the past, so why would he leave me now? I knew my situation was serious and could be life threatening, but God knew better than anyone else what was going to happen.

The next thing I did was get into my car, with my scooter in the back seat, and drove myself to church. I scooted into the church, sat down, and began to cry. I cried so long my eyes were swollen. After I got all my emotions out of my heart and didn't have another tear left, I sat there and prayed. I completely surrendered to God's will. I had lived fifty-eight years at that time, and I had tried to live my life as best I could, but if it was my time to go to my eternal home, I would be at peace with that and asked the Lord only for the strength to get through that time. I could not manage on my own, and I couldn't fall apart every day. I didn't want to scare my family, so I never showed them my deepest fear. I wanted to appear positive and strong. The more I kept that mindset, the more it became easy for me to live that way. You see, once I truly surrendered, I knew that God had it in His hands all along. Fear does not have a place in our heart when we have complete faith. I had always been so strong when I was faced with diversities in the past. There was no need to try to control what is meant to be.

Returning home after my time alone in the church, I became a more peaceful woman. I felt something spiritual had come over me to give me that peace. I released all my fears and worries to my God, and after that day I began to live my life as usual, just like the doctors said. I didn't just sit on the sofa; I had better things to do. I knew I was going to be stuck in a hospital after my surgery, and I already had been stuck in the house the last two months on the scooter because of my leg injury. I decided to simply live one day at a time and really embrace each day. Believe me, the month flew by because I wasn't dwelling on the fear. Instead, I walked in faith and had an inner knowing that God had this one. Before I knew it came the day I was to return to have my cast removed. It felt so good the day they freed my leg. After three months in the cast and wheeling around on that scooter, I could finally walk out of the doctor's office.

I don't think more than two days had gone by when I received a call from Mayo Clinic's cardiac surgery department. They were making plans to set up my open-heart surgery. I was scheduled to come in for my pre-op in a couple of days with my surgery scheduled to follow a week later. During that waiting period, I was not nervous at all, and it made me even more certain that something spiritual had come upon me that special afternoon I spent with God in the church. I'd asked for strength, and boy, did He ever give it to me.

I will never forget the day I went into the hospital for the big day. Jim drove me, my mother, and Linda to the Mayo Clinic in the early morning. Everyone was very quiet on the ride up, and I stayed in prayer, but not for myself. I was praying for all my family to have strength. I'd already found mine. As I checked in and sat in the waiting room with all three of them, Linda got so nervous she started to vomit. I took her off to the side and had a heart-to-heart talk with her. I asked her to pray with me, but she refused. She was still angry with God for the loss of her leg twenty-five years earlier. To believe that a higher being named God was watching over all of us was not something she could do. I then told her to be strong and that whatever happened, she needed to go on and raise those boys the best she could.

After I walked back to where my mother and husband sat, I talked to my mother. She was beside herself with worry, as any mother would be, and I so understood. She softened her ways the older she got, and I had forgiven her for the past. I told her I was in God's hands and what would be, would be. I never thought I could be so strong without emotionally falling apart. I then sat down and looked into my husband's eyes. No words needed to be said; we just sat and held hands. Before I knew it, the nurse was calling my name. It was my turn to take the step of faith into my own journey. I turned to kiss my daughter and then my mother, and then last, I kissed my husband, who had tears running down his face. I asked him to not cry. Then I took off my wedding band and handed it to him and asked him to give it back to me when I opened my eyes. I then turned on my heels toward the nurse, and off I went on my own spiritual walk, never turning around to look back. I just looked up and told God that I knew He had it covered. Whatever was to happen was God's will and I was at peace.

As I entered my hospital room, there was a team of people waiting on me, and at that time I simply broke down emotionally. "Why are there so many people in this room?" I asked. "I have been in surgery before but never experienced this type of treatment."

They answered that I had never had open-heart surgery and this was their process. I began shaking all over and knew I was experiencing a panic attack. I couldn't breathe. The human side was taking over my body. I was completely, out-of-my-mind afraid.

"Please give me something for this anxiety and please make it fast," I begged.

The anesthesiologist came in and talked to me before they administered something in my IV to calm me down. It brought me back to the place of calmness once again. My surgeon came in to see me just before they took me to the operating room. We talked and then he grabbed my hands and we prayed together. I was completely at ease when they rolled me through the doorway.

The next thing I remember was someone talking to me, calling me by name. *Oh my, is that you, God?* I thought. But no, it was the nurse. I had made it through my surgery, and I felt a tear run down my cheek. *Thank you, God.*

Soon after, I remember seeing my family again. They were crying and smiling at the same time. I saw my husband's face, and it looked like he had aged ten years in the hours I was in surgery. He smiled as he bent down to kiss me but had very few words. I think he was fighting back tears and was afraid of his own emotions right then. I was so out of it at that point, I could hardly keep my eyes open. I knew they had put me in a room and I was being hooked up to all types of machines with tubes and other things connected to me. I fell back into a kind of sleep. I could hear, but I couldn't make words come out of my mouth. All that mattered was that I'd made it.

I think it was the next day when I became more aware of what was going on. I was in tremendous pain. Oh, it was so bad! "Please help me," I begged the nurses. "I can't take the pain!" I cried. The nurses put pain medication in my IV, and then I was out again. I stayed in that state until the pain woke me once again. I couldn't take it. It was inhuman to have that much pain, I thought, and begged again for the nurses to please make it go away. But all they could do was give me more IV pain medicine, and out I would go again. I was trapped in my own body and couldn't move.

As the days went by, I was moved out of the ICU to a regular room. And at that time, I was encouraged to get out of bed and walk. I remember my daughter and son on either side of me as I walked the halls, pulling my IV holder along with me. I was so happy that my son had come to Florida for my surgery. He brought me his special rosary beads, the same rosary beads he'd put on his sister's bed when she was in the coma years before. I was now able to sit up and eat regular food. They had removed all the tubes from my chest, and it was only a matter of time until I would go home.

It was a little over eight days from the surgery until I was released from the hospital. I was given a red-heart pillow to hold on my chest when I would cough or move. And yes, I needed it; the pain was very intense for weeks. I think I had been home for a few days when my blood pressure got very high and I was having shortness of breath, so my husband took me to a local hospital. I went there first and stayed for three or four days while the Mayo Clinic was called and informed of my situation. I waited for four days until Mayo had a room for me and I was transported back to the facility in an ambulance. *Oh no. What's going on?* I thought.

That was such a scary time. They needed to get me back to the hospital to be checked to see whether my body was rejecting the new heart valve they'd installed or if I was possibly getting an infection. So many things raced through my mind as the ambulance sped along the highway, its lights flashing and sirens blaring. I hoped I was not dying.

Once back at Mayo, my surgeon came in to see me and ordered a series of tests. A few days later, after they got my blood levels and blood pressure back in check, they released me again. But I didn't want to go home. I was scared to death something was going to go wrong again. I forgot for that split moment that God had my back and that if I was going to die at that time, He would have already taken me. I had to return to the place of faith and peace. I heard a little voice telling me this was just a stumbling block and that I had to get it together and walk with my faith as I had always done.

Back at home, as I was sitting, lying down, or walking, the pain was horrible. The only relief was when I was taking the pain pills. I finally got a chance to see how Linda had felt when she took her pills. Not only do they take away the physical pain, but they numb the emotional pain, too. The more I took, the more I didn't care about anything. I just laid there, hoping and praying to get back to my new normality. I knew my life would never be the same again. In some ways, I knew it would be better and I would face it with a new sense of self and appreciation of life.

As the days passed, I had more time on my hands than I wanted, but as I sat, I began to think back on the cruise. The purpose of the cruise was to be a celebration of life for everything Linda had gone through in her life and for my mother after the loss of my father the year before. I thought that's what it was intended for, but God had another purpose for the trip. Little did I know at the time I planned that trip, I would come to find that it was God's way of letting me find my heart problem. The chain of events: I went zip lining only to hit a tree, only to break a leg, only to have to scoot around on a scooter for two months, only to get sick and have a CAT scan, only to find out I had an aneurysm in my heart. Had we not taken that cruise, and had that chain of events not taken place, I would not be here writing this book. God had a much bigger plan awaiting me. That's another miracle I had the opportunity to experience, and what a humbling feeling that was. I was in total gratitude.

I started with my in-house physical therapy, and by then I had nurses coming to the house three times a week. This process lasted for about a month. I was trying to get back my strength. I hadn't walked on both legs for over three months. So when I first got up to walk, I was very weak. But with each day and each week, I was getting back my strength. In a few months, I was somewhat back to normal. My blood was not staying very stable, however, and that was a problem. You see, when you have an artificial valve, you are limited as to what blood thinners you can take. Mine just so happened to be Coumadin, and that was a tough one to get used to. It took over a year and a half to become stable for me.

Then, just when I thought I was on the track to getting better, I began noticing nose bleeds. As they started to become more frequent, I contacted the doctors at Mayo and they recommended I keep a close handle on my blood levels. After replacement-valve heart surgery, it's very important to have routine blood testing to check what they call an INR (International Normalized Ratio) level in the blood, and it must stay within a certain range. My problem was that either my body wasn't reacting well to the blood thinner or I wasn't eating the right foods. You must understand that once on this pill, you have to watch your vitamin K: too much or too little can be a problem. I just ended up being one of the rare cases where the blood level was jumping back and forth in a dangerous area.

And that landed me in another surgery. I had hemorrhaged in my nose. What was supposed to be a routine checkup with an ENT (ear, nose, and throat) doctor at the Mayo Clinic ended up having me admitted into the hospital for immediate surgery the following morning. I had to call my husband to let him know. I sat in the hospital bed that day almost laughing and crying at the same time. "This is one sick joke, God—again?" I said to myself.

Well, I waited out the day as I had done so many times in the past. I was such a pro at hospital stays and surgeries I was not even scared. The next morning, Jim was there before I went to the operating room, and this time he was much calmer. I think he was getting adjusted to the routine I was going through. He kissed me, and off I went again. I was back before I knew it, and here comes the funny part: they had inserted what the medical field calls "rocket pockets" in my nose. Funny as the name is, the look of them is just as funny. They look like bloody tampons in your nose, each with a string taped to the side of your face. *You've got to be kidding me,* I thought when I looked in the mirror. And I had to wear them for two weeks. Well, I could take a joke, but that went way too far.

Once again, I had no choice, so I had another two weeks of isolation. I was not going to be seen in public with these things in my nose. By now, I was getting stir crazy. It seemed every time I tried to get back to work, something else showed up and I was back in the hospital.

I was losing track of the months, between my own health issues and taking care of Linda again and going back and forth to Mayo with her. We found out not only her liver was very bad, but her sugar was at its worst levels ever. They wanted to operate on her leg, but other issues were preventing the surgery. In the end, they just gave her more pain meds.

Also during that time, my mother was getting worse on her hip. She had fallen a few years back and ripped her muscle, and over the years it had gotten bad, so now we were awaiting her upcoming surgery.

Now, you're not going to believe this one, but with all these crazy health issues already going on in my family, my husband became deathly ill and we rushed him to the hospital. He was admitted with extreme vomiting, diarrhea, and stomach pain. After he was admitted into a hospital in Ormond Beach, the doctors diagnosed him a few days later with diverticulitis, gastritis, and a bleeding ulcer. It was a whirlwind. I couldn't comprehend all that at the same time. For goodness' sake, I was just getting better myself, and now I was visiting Jim every day in the hospital as well as looking in on my mother and Linda.

CHAPTER 10

One evening on my way home from the hospital, I noticed a little blood coming out of my nose. I never gave any thought to it; the doctors had said they'd repaired all the vessels in my nose, and I wasn't going to make a big thing out of it. I went to bed only to be awakened by a feeling of wetness on my face. I got up to look in the mirror to find I had hemorrhaged out of my nose, and this time it was bad. My face and hair were saturated with blood. I jumped in the shower and washed the blood off. When I was finished, it was about four a.m., and I hurriedly threw on some clothes, grabbed a bag of cotton balls and an empty baggy, and drove myself alone to the Mayo Clinic. I kept changing out the cotton balls as the blood filled them, putting the used ones in the empty baggy. I continued that process during my hour's drive to Mayo. By the time I got there, they called in a surgeon on call and decided to admit me immediately. They packed my nose, and the next day when my surgeon came in, they decided to do emergency surgery.

With my husband in one hospital and with me in another, I waited to call him. It was around ten o'clock that morning that I made the call. No words can describe the feelings we were having. He was helpless and wasn't going to be released, and I was scheduled for surgery the following morning. I couldn't cry; I couldn't do anything but sit. I didn't get it and probably never will—was this a joke, a curse? But I know one thing: it was not funny. My mother did surprise me, though, by having my sister bring her to the hospital to be there for me while I was in surgery. I was so surprised and very grateful to have her there. She stayed a couple of days until Jim was released from the hospital, and then he came to my hospital to stay with me one more day. I was released three days after my surgery.

    Once back at home, Jim seemed to be doing better. He was on a very bland, restricted diet. I had to watch my diet, too, because my INR blood levels had to stay within range or I could bleed out again. As I said, vitamin K could be my friend or my enemy, depending upon how much I consumed. I tend to lean on the high side of the acceptable number, and that means my blood is too thin, which could lead to another hemorrhage.

My Unexpected Journey

As the holidays approached, we went along as if everything was just fine. In fact, it was for the most part. Jim and I promised that we would ring in the New Year with a bang. Out with the old and in with the new. For the brand-new year, we vowed to stay healthy and prayed to stay out of hospitals. Unfortunately, that didn't exactly work well. A few days after Christmas, Jim became deathly ill again, and that time was worse than the last. I rushed him to the hospital, where we learned his gastritis and bleeding ulcer were acting up. He couldn't stop vomiting, and the pain was uncontrollable. Subsequently, we spent New Year's in the hospital, and he was released three days later.

It was then the beginning of January, with Jim home from the hospital and time for my mother's hip surgery. My sister and I drove her to the hospital and were with her the day of her surgery. I also decided to stay with her for the night while Judy headed back home. They said my mother would be able to leave the following day if all went well. Although I didn't tell anyone because all of the sickness we had been through, I had been feeling odd myself over the last few weeks. I felt I couldn't breathe very well, and when I walked, I was having a problem with pain in my hip and my back, even in the hospital. So my sister ended up putting me in a wheelchair and pushing me to my mother's room. I came to find out much later that the pain in my hip was due to tear in it from a fall I'd had a few months back. It was causing the shortness of breath and weakness, as well.

Once my mother was back home, my sister and I tried to get home health care for her because she was not to put any weight on her hip for three months. Both my sister and I had jobs, and we tried so many times to hire help to come to the house, but my mother fought us tooth and nail about it. She didn't want outside help and was crying that she didn't have any family to take care of her, and she was feeling very sorry for herself. She knew how to tweak us by always using the guilt card, and she played that card very well. One night I would sleep with her, and the next night my sister would spend the night. We tried to hire caregivers from four or five different services to come in and take care of her, but each time, she fired them and said she could take care of herself. But of course that was not possible. She was in a wheelchair with a massive brace on her right leg, for goodness' sake. We kept explaining to her that we couldn't take care of her alone, that we needed outside help.

I was running around out of control and mostly not taking care of myself. It had been weeks since I'd checked my blood, which should have been tested weekly. One night when I was sleeping in my mother's bed, I was awakened by the worst headache I've ever experienced. I felt ill, but I just took a few Tylenols and went on my way.

The next day, I received a call from my grandson, who said my daughter was doing very badly and that I should come over right away. I quickly drove from my mother's house to Linda's house, only to indeed find her very sick and weak. She was very dehydrated, and her blood glucose levels were over the top. I pleaded with her to get to the emergency room to be checked, and once we got to the hospital, I was getting much sicker and my headache did not feel normal. I shrugged it off as a stress reaction. My grandson even ran to a nearby gas station to buy some more Tylenol for me. Nothing was working. As we awaited the outcome of Linda's bloodwork and test results, they decided to keep her. She was now in a dangerous situation with the sugar levels.

After we got her admitted, I took the boys home. At that point, they were sixteen and fifteen years old and they didn't want to come to my house. They live about a mile from me and are very responsible, so I let them stay home alone. When I returned to my own home, I was extremely ill. I could hardly see clearly. My husband took out my blood machine and tested my INR levels. It showed a 6.7 level—a normal level for a person with a heart-valve replacement is 2 to 2.5.

Something was happening to me, and it wasn't good. Jim rushed me to the same hospital to which Linda had just been admitted. A CAT scan was immediately performed on my brain, and it showed my problem to be a brain bleed. I was immediately given blood plasma through an IV and an injection of vitamin K. I was also informed that I would have to be transferred to another hospital because they were not able to treat me effectively at the current one.

An ambulance showed up very soon after that, and I was taken to the Ormond Beach Hospital. I was so scared. *Oh no, another ambulance ride with the lights on!* I was crying, and this time more than last time, I was afraid I was going to die. I had no idea what it meant to have a brain bleed. And I was now in an ambulance for a second time, being rushed to the hospital with something life threatening. I couldn't seem to wake out of my nightmare. I didn't even know how to pray at that point. I went totally blank and felt like I was coming in and out of consciousness. I was not taken to the ER but instead directly to the ICU. *This can't be good,* I thought to myself. I heard the nurses vaguely talking to me, but I could barely comprehend what was happening. With my heart beating out of control, I knew my blood pressure was way off the charts. *I know I am dying this time. Lord, why? I asked for your mercy. I can't do this anymore; I can't take it. I can't care for everyone and take care of myself. This is too much. Am I failing?*

I felt like it was the end. For the first time, I felt like I was going to die. I had no real life left inside me. I was a walking zombie. I had done my best for everyone, and now my own body was breaking down and I couldn't even help myself. Did I have any fight left? No, not at the exact moment. I wanted it to be over. My mind and body were overwrought to the point of exhaustion.

Just take me home now, Lord. Let this nightmare be over.

I kept my eyes shut and only answered the nurses and doctors when asked a question. I had so many IVs running through my veins I felt I was truly dying. I saw more nurses in my room than I had seen during my open-heart surgery, and I knew that couldn't be good. They gave me pain medication for my headache and another medication for my anxiety. That kept me in the zone where I wanted to stay. *Let me go out peacefully,* I thought.

The next thing I remember was the following day. I woke to a nurse taking my vitals and talking to me. "What happened?

And why am I here?" I asked. She explained that I was brought in during the night before because I'd had a brain bleed due to my INR levels being too elevated. My blood had become too thin and had broken through into the cranial cavity at the base of the brain. Two centimeters of blood had seeped into my brain before they could stop the bleeding. My brain was no longer bleeding, she explained, and they were now in the process of watching to see if the blood in the brain would dissolve itself without surgery.

I met with the brain surgeon later that day, and he explained the whole process in more detail. Thankfully, I was in a better state of mind by the time he talked with me. In my mind, I figured if I was going to die I would have died the night before. So now, he said, we had decisions and options to talk about, and I was listening very carefully as he explained my options and what he felt was in my best interest.

They were taking CAT scans of my brain every couple of days to make sure no more blood was seeping into my brain. But on the flip side was the fact that since they stopped the bleeding, now my blood was too thick. At the same time, my INR levels were less than acceptable. I was at a stroke level. A normal person's blood level is 1.0. I was at a 1.1 level with a heart valve (I should have levels between 2.0 and 2.5), which meant I could have had a stroke at any time. It was a double-edged knife: blood in the brain and blood too thick for the heart valve to work correctly.

While I stayed in the ICU, the hospital medical staff were trying to get my blood levels up to a normal range without causing another major bleed out in some other part of my body. To sum this up, it took eleven days to get my blood levels back to a healthy range before I was permitted to leave.

During my eleven-day stay in the hospital, I had a lot of time to reflect on my life. I was alone most of the time without much company. But I found that during that time, as I was reading the Bible, I was inspired by God to write this book. I feel all that had happened to me throughout my life and especially during that year and a half had a deep purpose. I never thought I was capable of writing a book, especially one about my own life, but this came to me loud and clear: "Write your story! Tell others. Share your experiences to help those who need to hear this, and be there to help others."

Well, let me tell you, I thought the medications were making me crazy, first of all. *Me? Write a book? Yeah, sure,* I thought. But the feeling would not go away. So after I returned home, I decided to sit down and write this book to share my life experiences, to use my serious and challenging trials in life to help others overcome theirs.

Whatever we face in life, whether large or small, has an impact on how we feel and react. I want to thank you for reading my story, and I hope that reading about my journey can help you realize that whatever you are going through today is just a temporary obstacle. I am not saying it is easy, but it is not impossible to overcome.

Jackie Dobrosky

CHAPTER 11

I was so grateful to be able to leave that hospital and walk out after an eleven-day stay. And as I write this book, I can say that it has been months since I have had to visit a hospital.

Since that episode, my health has been improving every day, and I am sure to remind myself that I can't give more of myself than I have inside me. I learned all too well that if you put others ahead of your own self or health, you will not be good for anyone or anything. I gave up my martyr-and-victim role. I know it's difficult to change your mindset—it took me a long time to change mine—but I just made up my mind and did it. Not everyone is going to like you when you choose a course of action like that, and that's okay. I have found people-pleasers are sometimes the unhappiest people around because at times they feel obligated to do for others at the sake of their own health or happiness. God wants us to set healthy boundaries. That is not wrong. We are supposed to take care of ourselves and then if we can, help others.

Throughout my whole life I had been taking care of everyone else, even at the risk of my own life. And of course I am still Jackie, the person who will always be there when the chips are down for my friends and family. But the difference is this: it won't be at the sake of my own health, and now I know my limits. I must always be aware of them for the rest of my life.

Something I've found helpful to keep in mind is what the flight attendants instruct passengers on an airplane before takeoff: "In the event of a problem, always secure your own oxygen mask before helping others with theirs." And the same goes with life. We only have one life, and as children of the Lord, this is not selfish in any way. I had to learn the hard way. It took me almost losing my own life to take *back* my life.

I have been healing physically and emotionally for the past two years, beginning even before my sickness. I am still a work in progress, and every day I become a stronger woman in spite of the past. I came back from what I feel was the depths of hell and am here to tell you anyone can overcome their own adversities, small or large. Whether they are health problems, bad relationships, addictions, financial difficulties, divorce, death of a loved one, or abuse of any sort, you can get through them. I have dealt with all of those; it wasn't easy, it still isn't, but now I am aware. And when I am faced with those challenges again, I have learned to handle them differently. None of us will ever be without some sort of problems; that's just life. I just try to see my daggers before they stab me and to avoid situations that create more drama.

Finally, I look at this Jackie today, a woman in her sixties, and for the first time in all her life, free to live the life she always wanted and deserved, free from drama, dysfunction, and control. I became a friend to this Jackie. I like her—with all of her imperfections that she earned on her way through to this point. I accept all of her faults and have learned so much from the mistakes because in reality, they weren't mistakes at all but lessons from which she had to learn and grow.

As my journey is not finished, every day I wake up is a new day to be alive, and I embrace what lies ahead. I will handle things as they come. I don't dwell too much on the *what ifs*. They will drive you crazy.

There is nothing that life gives us that we can't get through.

I am now focusing on my health and most importantly my husband and our marriage, which for more than the last three-and-a-half years has taken a back seat to all that has happened since our wedding. I want to spend the rest of our days focusing on each other. It took me many years to find my "Mr. Right." I am blessed that he has weathered the storm with me since our wedding. God willing, we will be able to share many happy years together.

ABOUT THE AUTHOR

Author and motivational speaker Jackie Dobrosky has been inspired to help energize others to find the hope and strength they need to face any of life's challenges. An Ohio native, Jackie now resides in Florida with her husband, Jim. She enjoys the Florida lifestyle, entertaining friends, and traveling.

www.ingramcontent.com/pod-product-compliance
Lightning Source LLC
Chambersburg PA
CBHW071559080526
44588CB00010B/961